give-it-away
crafts
for kids

Group

Loveland, Colorado

www.group.com

Give-It-Away Crafts for Kids

Copyright © 2005 Group Publishing, Inc.

Visit our Web site: **www.group.com**

Credits

Contributing Authors: Gwyn D. Borcherding, Sharon Carey, Teryl Cartwright, Lorie A. Erhard, Jan Kershner, Julie Lavender, Jennifer Nystrom, Larry Shallenberger, and Bonnie Temple
Editor: Scott M. Kinner
Creative Development Editor: Mikal Keefer
Chief Creative Officer: Joani Schultz
Copy Editor: Jessica Broderick
Art Director: Becky Hawley Design, Inc.
Designer: Becky Hawley Design, Inc.
Print Production Artist: Becky Hawley Design, Inc.
Illustrator: Sharon Holm
Production Manager: Peggy Naylor

Library of Congress Cataloging-in-Publication Data

Give-it-away crafts for kids.
    p. cm.
 Includes index.
 ISBN 0-7644-2768-7 (pbk. : alk. paper)
 1. Bible crafts. I. Group Publishing.

 BS613.G58 2004
 268'.432--dc22

                        2004015700

10 9 8 7 6 5 4 3 2 1   14 13 12 11 10 09 08 07 06 05

Printed in the United States of America.

Group resources actually work!

This Group resource helps you focus on **"The 1 Thing™"**— a life-changing relationship with Jesus Christ. "The 1 Thing" incorporates our **R.E.A.L.** approach to ministry. It reinforces a growing friendship with Jesus, encourages long-term learning, and results in life transformation, because it's:

Relational
Learner-to-learner interaction enhances learning and builds Christian friendships.

Experiential
What learners experience through discussion and action sticks with them up to 9 times longer than what they simply hear or read.

Applicable
The aim of Christian education is to equip learners to be both hearers and doers of God's Word.

Learner-based
Learners understand and retain more when the learning process takes into consideration how they learn best.

Table of Contents

Section 3: Friends

Section 4: Those in Need

Section 5: The Community

Bible Point Index

Bible Verse Index

Introduction

You've worked so hard to find a great craft idea, searching through craft book after craft book. You've been to the supply closet to gather materials enough times that you're considering pitching a tent in there. You want kids to create something memorable, something that reinforces learning. But it happens again, just as it has in the past: When you walk out of the building, you see the latest creation in a trash can near the door.

No teacher enjoys discovering that crafts created in the classroom never made it past the parking lot.

That won't happen with *Give-It-Away Crafts for Kids* because these fifty-two crafts are designed to be given away as outreach or encouragement. Some of the crafts won't even make it *to* the parking lot because they'll be handed to the pastor, the Christian education director, or even the church custodian.

There are two main goals we wanted to accomplish with these crafts.

❶ Real Learning. There's little educational benefit in making a craft for the sake of making a craft. But when the craft reinforces a Bible point or leads to the application of Bible truth, it becomes a powerful teaching tool.

Each craft reinforces and references a Bible truth (a Bible story or a Bible topic), so there's always learning happening when crafts are created. They're fun, but they're fun with a purpose!

❷ Giving to Others. Kids will not only be proud of their work in the class but will also be able to share it with others. Each craft is designed to be given away to one of these five categories of people and places:

- **church staff and volunteers**—where foam mouse-pad creations remind the office staff of the lives they are changing, even with menial tasks;

- **family**—where a simple chocolate gift can communicate love and send a message that someone cares;

- **friends**—where a yo-yo can launch a fun, lifelong relationship;

- **those in need**—where a cushioned encouragement card cheers up someone in a local hospice and communicates the love of Jesus; and

- **the community**—where a badge of courage given to a police officer or a simple mobile to hang over a dentist's chair can be used for outreach and community involvement.

The projects are even arranged by category, so you can easily find a craft for a different area in which to reach out and serve. Or if you need something to make a Bible point or reinforce a Bible passage, check the indexes in the back.

We call these fifty-two projects *crafts* because they are created by children, but it's probably more appropriate to refer to them as child-sized service projects. As children unleash their creativity, it's a great time to sneak in some lifelong learning…and serve others.

Creation Shakers

Bible Point

God is the Creator of everything!

Scripture

"Do you not know? Have you not heard? The Lord is the everlasting God, the Creator of the ends of the earth" (Isaiah 40:28a).

Making this craft will remind kids that God is their Creator and creation is evidence of his great love for us. With each twist, turn, or tip of the jar, creation items will appear to remind us that our Creator is amazing and wonderful.

Supplies

- clean, empty baby food jars or clear plastic soda bottles
- craft sand or raw white rice
- permanent markers
- small items representing creation, such as seashells and small artificial flowers
- colored electrical tape (optional)

Steps

1. Have each child write the words "The Lord is the Creator" on the outside of a jar with permanent marker.

2. Allow kids to select several of the creation items and put them in their jars.

3. Have kids fill the jars about two-thirds full with the sand.

4. Put the lids on the jars, and help kids tape them in place with colored electrical tape.

Closing

Discuss these questions with your children:

- **What are your favorite things in creation?**

- **How does creation show us God's love?**

- **How can we use creation to tell others that God loves them?**

- **How would this craft help someone grow closer to God?**

Say: **Sometimes we forget that God is with us and that he loves us. When we take time to notice things in creation, it helps us feel closer to God. Let's give our crafts to someone on the church staff. Sometimes our church leaders face big problems and heavy responsibilities. These Creation Shakers can remind them of God's love and power, put a smile on their faces, and help them remember why they've chosen to serve God's people!**

Pray: **Dear Lord, thank you for loving us so much and for giving us such great and cool things in creation. We praise you for being a powerful, amazing, and fun-loving Creator! Refresh our church leaders, and draw them close to you. In Jesus' name, amen.**

Faithful Weather Vanes

Bible Point

We can always trust God to lead us.

Scripture

"Now faith is being sure of what we hope for and certain of what we do not see" (Hebrews 11:1).

Many church staff members don't get to see the fruits of their labor. This craft will not only help children understand the meaning of faith but will also help church staff and volunteers remember that their faith in the Lord helps others grow in relationship with Jesus.

Supplies

- card stock
- plastic straws cut in half
- safety scissors
- markers or crayons
- clear tape
- large paper clips

Before Craft

Cut the card stock into 1x5-inch rectangles and 6-inch squares. You'll need one rectangle and one square for each child.

Steps

1. Give each child a paper clip, a square, a rectangle, and a plastic straw half.

2. Explain that a weather vane has a large, flat shape called an ornament that is designed to catch wind. Have each child use markers and safety scissors to design an ornament and cut it from the rectangle.

3. Direct kids to tape their straws to the middle of their ornaments so that the straw and ornament are perpendicular. The straw should extend below the ornament about two or three inches.

④ Show the children how to bend their paper clips into an L shape. The small end of each paper clip should be totally straightened and stand straight up. The large end will remain bent for the base. Have kids tape this end to the card-stock squares.

⑤ Have the children put together their weather vanes by setting the bottom of their straws over the standing-up portion of the paper-clip bases. Show the children how to blow on the ornament to make it turn.

Closing

Discuss these questions with your children:

- **How do we know there is wind when we can't see it?**

- **What are some other things we know exist that we can't see?**

- **How do we know that God loves us, even though we can't see him?**

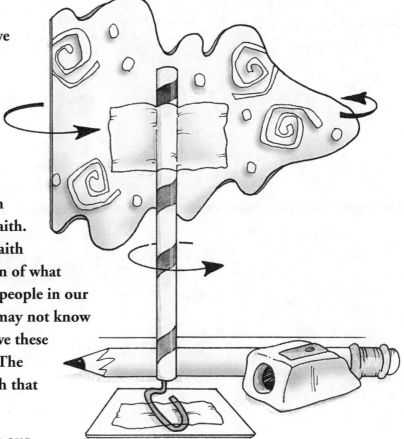

Say: **When we know something for sure even though we can't see it, that means we have faith. The Bible tells us what faith means: "Now faith is being sure of what we hope for and certain of what we do not see" (Hebrews 11:1). Every week people in our church help us know Jesus better, but they may not know if they're really making a difference. Let's give these weather vanes to the leaders in our church. The weather vanes will remind them to have faith that they're making a difference.**

Pray: **Dear God, thank you for the leaders in our church who help us know you better. Help them to be strong in their faith. In Jesus' name, amen.**

Footprints of Faith

Bible Point

Walk humbly with God.

Scripture

"He has showed you, O man, what is good. And what does the Lord require of you? To act justly and to love mercy and to walk humbly with your God" (Micah 6:8).

These footprint reminders will encourage people to walk humbly with God and to show his mercy to others.

Supplies

- colored folders
- markers and crayons
- safety scissors
- hole punch
- at least two 16-inch lengths of yarn or leather lacing per child
- Bible

Steps

1. Set out a variety of colored folders. Have kids cut different shoe shapes, as viewed from the top, from the colored folders. Tell kids they can trace around their own shoes if they'd like to. (Kids should be able to make a complete pair of shoes from one folder.) Encourage kids to cut shapes for running shoes, hiking boots, high heels, ballet slippers, and so on.

2. Have kids use crayons and markers to decorate each shape to look like the type of shoe it represents. For example, they could draw treads on the hiking boot shape and straps on the high heel.

3. Help kids use a hole punch to make shoelace holes in each shape. Let kids lace their paper shoes with yarn, leather, or actual shoelaces.

4 Have kids each use a fine-tipped marker to write "Walk humbly with God" on their shoe shapes.

Closing

Help kids find Micah 6:8, and ask a volunteer to read the passage out loud. Then discuss these questions with your children:

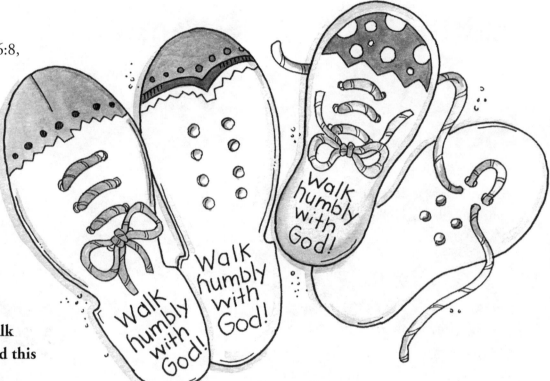

- **What does it mean to be humble?**

- **What does this verse say to you?**

- **How can you walk humbly with God this week?**

Say: **God tells us how to please him— by showing mercy and fairness and by not showing off or trying to act better than anyone else. We're going to decorate our church with these shoe shapes so everyone can be reminded to walk humbly with God wherever we go.**

Tape the shoes to different locations in your church. Tell kids that they can make the same shoes at home to remind their families to walk humbly with God too!

Pray: **Dear Lord, thank you for showing us how to please you. Help us to be humble, and help us not to be stuck on ourselves. Help us, please, to remember to trust you and walk humbly with you every day. In Jesus' name, amen.**

"God Is Faithful" Banners

Bible Point

God is faithful to us all.

Scripture

"For the Lord is good and his love endures forever; his faithfulness continues through all generations" (Psalm 100:5).

Your church is made up of people from all generations. But they have one thing in common—God is faithful to them all! These banners will remind people who come into your church that God loves them and is faithful.

Supplies

- old magazines
- safety scissors
- glue
- wax paper
- construction paper
- markers and crayons
- one 3-foot length of yarn per child
- Bible

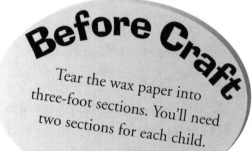

Before Craft

Tear the wax paper into three-foot sections. You'll need two sections for each child.

Steps

1. Let kids use old magazines to cut out pictures of people of all ages, from babies to senior citizens.

2. Explain that each child will use the pictures to make a collage between two sheets of wax paper. Demonstrate how to glue the pictures on one sheet and run a thin line of glue all around the edge of the wax paper. Have kids place the other sheet on top and seal the edges.

3 Fold a sheet of construction paper in half lengthwise. Show kids how to fold it over the top of the collage.

4 Show kids how to lay a length of yarn inside the fold. Then have them glue the construction paper in place and tie the ends of the yarn together to form hangers.

5 Help kids write the words of Psalm 100:5 on the construction-paper tops of their banners.

Closing

Discuss these questions with your children:

- **How could you say this verse in your own words?**

- **How has God shown his love and faithfulness to you?**

- **Look at the pictures on your banner. How does God show his faithfulness at different stages of life?**

Say: **God loves everyone, and he's faithful to all generations. He loves babies, kids your age, teenagers, young adults, and people your grandparents' age. God is faithful to us all! We'll hang our banners in the church entrance to remind everyone who comes in the door that God is faithful to us all! Let's thank God right now for his love for us.**

Pray: **Dear God, thank you so much for loving us. Thank you for being faithful to us all, no matter how young or old we are. Help us to be thankful and to share your love with others this week. In Jesus' name, amen.**

God's Garden of Love

Bible Point

God will always be there for us.

Scripture

"But there is a friend who sticks closer than a brother" (Proverbs 18:24b).

A flower is such a wonderful picture of God's love for us. Its delicate beauty and fragrance touch our senses and remind us that God is a loving creator. This craft will give children a beautiful garden to share with your church and remind your kids that God created them, too—and God loves them!

Supplies

- 6 tissue-paper circles of different colors per child, 2 of each size (9 inch, 7 inch, and 5 inch)
- 1 chenille wire per child
- one 2x3-inch leaf cut from green construction paper per child
- tape
- bulletin board or large piece of newsprint

Steps

1. Give each child six tissue-paper circles, a chenille wire, and a leaf. Instruct kids to write their names on their leaves.

2. Direct kids to place the two small circles on top of the two medium circles. Then place those four circles on top of the two large circles. Have kids make a U out of the chenille wire, then push both ends through all six layers of tissue paper about a half inch apart. The ends will stick out beneath the largest circles. Kids will then twist the chenille wire together to form the stem of their flowers. Show children how to fold up each circle to create a ruffle of petals.

3. Give the children each a piece of tape, and have kids tape their leaves onto the stems by folding the tape

around the stem, sandwiching the leaf in between the ends of the tape.

 Place a bulletin board or piece of newsprint in your hallway, and write the words "God's Garden of Love" at the top of the board or paper. Help children attach their flowers with additional tape.

Closing

Discuss these questions with your children:

- **How do we know that God is always with us?**

- **What kinds of things remind us of God's love for us?**

- **How can we help remind each other that God loves us all?**

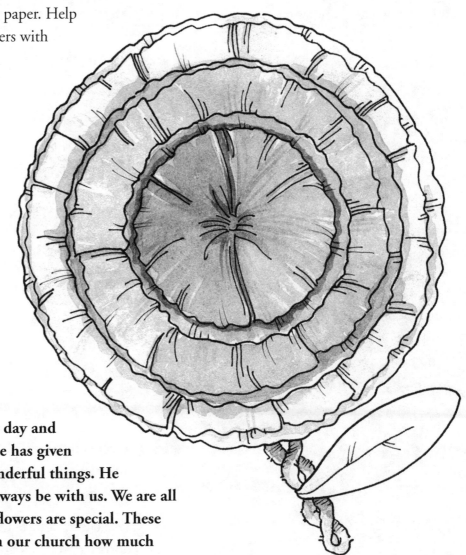

Say: **We can look around every day and see how much God loves us. He has given us a great big world full of wonderful things. He has promised us that he will always be with us. We are all special in his eyes, just as our flowers are special. These flowers can remind everyone in our church how much God loves us and that he will always be with us.**

Pray: **Dear Jesus, thank you for always being with us. Thank you for giving us all the beautiful things in this world to remind us of that. We're so glad you love us. In Jesus' name, amen.**

Hug for You

Bible Point

God wants us to show love.

Scripture

"Dear children, let us not love with words or tongue but with actions and in truth" (1 John 3:18).

In 1 John 3:18, we are reminded that God wants us to show our love through our actions in addition to our words. With this craft, children will remind church staff members that they are loved, cared for, and appreciated.

Supplies

- construction paper in a variety of colors, especially red
- markers
- safety scissors
- tape
- Hershey's Hugs candies
- Bible

Steps

1. Give each child four or five pieces of construction paper. Help each child cut out a large heart from a sheet of construction paper. Have kids each draw a face on their hearts.

2. Direct children to cut four 6-inch strips of construction paper and tape the strips to the sides of the heart to form arms and legs.

3. Have children trace their hands and feet onto construction paper and cut out the shapes. Help the children tape the hand cutouts to the strips that form the arms. Then have them tape their feet cutouts to the strips that form the legs.

4. Help children write the words of 1 John 3:18 and "Consider yourself hugged" on the back of their hearts.

 Give each child one Hershey's Hugs candy to tape to the inside of both hands, as if the heart character is holding the candy.

Closing

Discuss these questions with your children:

- **How do you use your words to let someone know you love him or her?**

- **What can you do, without using words, to show someone you love him or her?**

- **Can you tell me how you've used your actions to show your love?**

Say: **It's always nice to feel loved, especially for people who work in our church and help us grow closer to Jesus. God wants us to use our actions to show his love and our love to others. Before you leave church today, share your craft with a worker to remind him or her of your love and appreciation.**

Pray: **Dear God, thank you for the people in our church who share your love with us. Help us remind them that we love them, too. In Jesus' name, amen.**

Tip

Many children may want to give their hearts to you. Encourage kids to share their crafts with several other people so that many servants in your church have the opportunity to feel a dose of affirmation.

Pocket Full of Prayers

Bible Point

God answers the prayers of his children.

Scripture

"The prayer of a righteous man is powerful and effective" (James 5:16b).

Have you ever waited at the window for a friend or relative to arrive for a visit? You wanted to know when they arrived so you could run and tell the rest of your family. We can watch for God's answers to our prayers in the same way we watch for a friend. The Bible tells us that God hears when his children pray. Watching for God's answers builds our faith and helps us be thankful. Children will create prayer wallets in which to keep prayer requests and answers. By sharing them, they will encourage others to pray and watch for God's answers.

Supplies

- one 5½ x11-inch piece of vinyl wallpaper per child
- markers or crayons
- stapler
- 6 index cards per child
- Bible

Steps

1 Give each child a piece of wallpaper, and instruct kids to fold the pieces in half, making squares. Have kids open the squares and make a two-inch fold on both ends to create the pockets.

2 Help kids staple the sides of the pockets close to the edges.

3 Tell kids to open the wallets and neatly write "Prayer Requests" on one pocket of each wallet. On the other pocket, have them write "Answers."

4 Help kids find James 5:16b and write the passage on the outside of their wallets.

5 Direct kids to insert the index cards into the "Requests" pocket.

Closing

Discuss these questions with your children:

- **What does this verse tell us about the prayers of a person who is righteous?**

- **How does that make you feel about prayer?**

- **What can you pray for today?**

Say: **God has promised to hear and answer the prayers of those who love him. Whenever we pray, we should watch for God's answers. Sometimes he answers with a "yes" and sometimes with a "no," but he always answers with "I love you." Give your craft to someone in our church today to help that person remember different prayer requests. Remind the person that God makes our prayers strong, and pray with that person.**

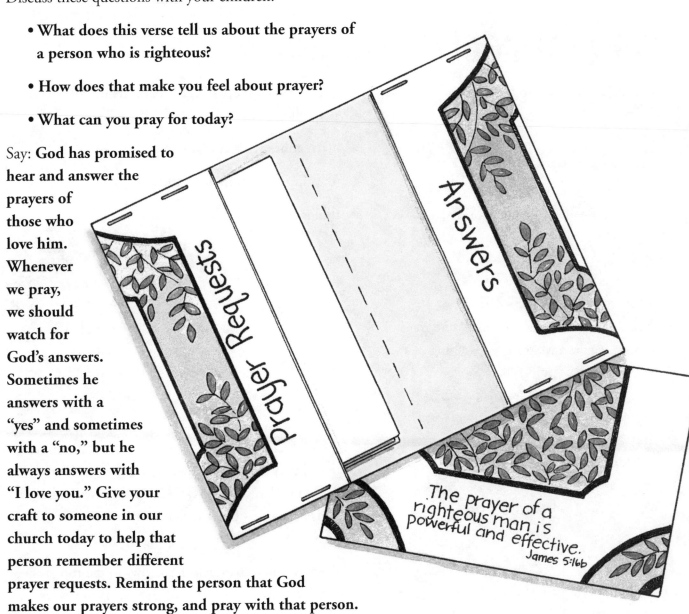

Pray: **Dear Jesus, thank you for hearing all our prayers. Help us watch for the way you answer each one. In Jesus' name, amen.**

Point-Click-Pray: Jesus Is the Way

Bible Point

Jesus points the way to God.

Scripture

"Jesus answered, 'I am the way and the truth and the life. No one comes to the Father except through me'" (John 14:6).

On the Internet, point, click, and in seconds we have what we're searching for. In life, Jesus points us to God. Children will create a mouse pad to remind someone that Jesus points us to God, and in God, we find what we're searching for.

Supplies

- one 7x9-inch piece of craft foam in any color per child
- black adhesive craft foam
- fine-tipped permanent markers
- Bible

Before Craft
Cut a 1½-inch arrow for each child out of the adhesive-backed craft foam. The arrow should resemble a computer arrow.

Steps

1. Give each child a 7x9-inch piece of craft foam. Have the children write in large letters at the top, "Point-Click-Pray: Jesus Is the Way." Help them write the words of John 14:6 in smaller, neat letters at the bottom.

2. Direct children to attach the arrows to the top corner of the craft foam, pointing to the words they wrote.

Closing

Discuss these questions with your children:

- **How is an arrow on a computer screen helpful?**

• In what way does Jesus point us to heaven?

• How can a relationship with Jesus show the way to God?

Say: **Arrows point to important things and help us find our way. We need to know the way to heaven, and Jesus points us in the only direction to get there. He said, "I am the way and the truth and the life. No one comes to the Father except through me" (John 14:6). This means the only way we get to live in heaven with God forever is to have a friendship with Jesus. As we get to know Jesus better every day, he points us to God by teaching us how to live for him. Before you leave church today, give this craft to someone in the church office. It's a great reminder for everyone to focus on a relationship with Jesus.**

Pray: **Dear Jesus, thank you for pointing us to heaven and making the way for us to be with you there. Help us remember that you are the way, the truth, and the life. In Jesus' name, amen.**

Point·Click·Pray

Jesus Is the Way

"Jesus answered, 'I am the way and the truth and the life. No one comes to the Father except through me.'"
John 14:6

Presence Posies

Bible Point

Jesus, God's living word, is with us.

Scripture

"In the beginning was the Word, and the Word was with God, and the Word was God" (John 1:1).

Sometimes we forget that Jesus is always with us. Your children will create flower bouquets to share with church staff members. The bouquets will be a reminder that Jesus is always with us.

Supplies

- 2 unsharpened pencils per child
- 2 uninflated green balloons per child
- hole punch
- safety scissors
- permanent markers
- pastel-colored felt
- Bible

Before Craft

Cut the felt into 1½ x 9½-inch strips. You'll need two strips per child.

Steps

1. Help kids write the words of John 1:1 on the felt strips with markers, making sure the ink stays off kids' clothes.

2. Have kids cut one inch off the open end of each balloon. Show kids how to slide one cut-off end balloon piece up each pencil, thicker end toward the eraser. Direct kids to loosely wrap a felt strip around the eraser end of each pencil, allowing the edge to go lower each time around.

3 Ask kids to help each other by pinching the bottom of the felt "rosebud" while the other person pulls the thick part of the balloon piece over the felt bud at the bottom to hold the flower's shape.

4 Have kids punch two holes vertically in each balloon as shown.

5 Show kids how to fold over the balloon so the two holes line up and thread the balloon onto the pencil through the holes. Have kids move the balloon "leaf" to the middle of the pencil and press down on the center of the balloon to deflate slightly.

Closing

Say: **The verse we wrote on our crafts says that Jesus has been with God since creation—since God first created flowers and people. We created a flower bouquet as a reminder that Jesus is present with us all the time, just as he has been present since the beginning of creation.**

Ask: • **How do we know that Jesus is with us?**

• **Why do you think Jesus is always with us?**

Say: **Give your flower bouquet to someone who works in our church. Think about how *you* know that Jesus is with you, and share this with the church staff member who you give your flowers to.**

Pray: **Jesus, thank you for being with us. Help us to see you in creation and in every part of our lives. Amen.**

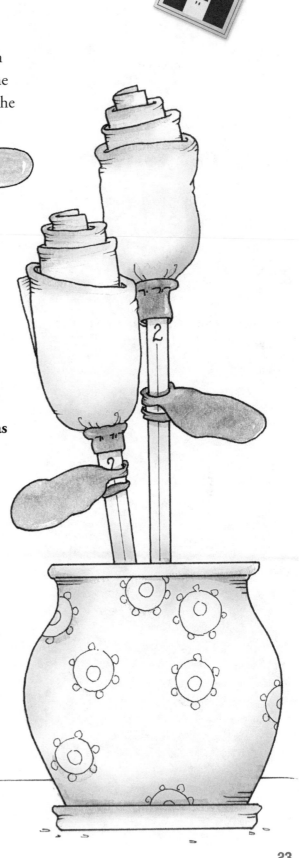

Rings Like Eagles

Bible Point

God keeps us going even when the going gets tough.

Scripture

"Those who hope in the Lord will renew their strength. They will soar on wings like eagles; they will run and not grow weary, they will walk and not be faint" (Isaiah 40:31).

Serving the Lord isn't always easy. Sometimes we get tired! With this craft, children will encourage church workers to remember to hope in the Lord and soar on eagles' wings.

Supplies

- eight 2⅞-inch-square self-stick notes of any color per child
- glue or stapler
- markers

Steps

1 Have kids fold all of their eight self-stick squares in half. The adhesive side will be on the inside of the fold.

2 When kids have finished folding the squares in half, show them how to fold each one in the following way. With the first fold at the top, fold down the upper-left corner and line it up with the bottom edges.
Then fold up the lower-right corner so its edges meet the top fold. You now have a parallelogram. Before you take your fingers off the paper, draw a dot on the right tip of the parallelogram.
(Note: For assembly, it's important to get the dot on the triangle with open flaps. The other triangle forms a pocket.)

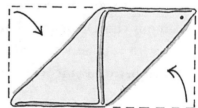

3 Help kids fold and dot all their pieces of paper.

4 To assemble the flying ring, help kids fit the dotted point of one parallelogram into the pocketed point (the undotted side) of another parallelogram. Continue working clockwise to make a circle.

5 To hold the sections of their rings in place, kids can staple or glue each section.

6 Have kids decorate their rings by writing some of the main words from the verse, such as *hope*, *renew*, *strength*, *run*, *walk*, *soar*, and *wings*, on both sides of their flying rings. Give kids an opportunity to try out the flying rings.

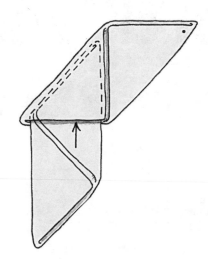

Closing

Discuss these questions with your children:

- **When have you gotten tired from doing something hard?**

- **How does God help you do even the toughest things?**

- **How can you help others renew their strength to do a hard job?**

Say: **God understands that sometimes working hard, even for him, can get tiring. That's why he made such a great promise to us in Isaiah 40:31: "Those who hope in the Lord will renew their strength. They will soar on wings like eagles; they will run and not grow weary, they will walk and not be faint." Give your craft to someone at church who works hard for Jesus, and tell that person that the flying ring will help him or her remember that God always renews our strength when we hope in him.**

Pray: **Jesus, thank you for understanding us so well. We want to encourage others to renew their strength in you. Amen.**

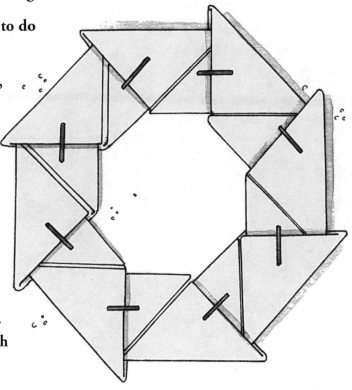

"Working for the Lord" Pins

Bible Point

Do everything for God.

Scripture

"Whatever you do, work at it with all your heart, as working for the Lord, not for men" (Colossians 3:23).

This heart-shaped pin will be a great reminder to work wholeheartedly for the Lord. When we work for the Lord with all our hearts, our Christlike intentions and our love for Jesus show through us.

Supplies

- 1 wooden die-cut heart per child
- bright-colored markers
- bright-colored puffy paint
- 1 self-adhesive pin clasp per child

Tip

Die-cut heart shapes can be purchased at a low cost at any craft store.

Steps

1. Distribute one wooden die-cut heart to each child, and have kids decorate the wooden hearts with markers.

2. Help the kids write "I'm working for the Lord" on the front with puffy paint and decorate as desired.

3. Direct kids to attach a pin clasp to the back of each heart.

Closing

Discuss these questions with your children:

- **What does it mean to work for the Lord with all our hearts?**

- **When we work for the Lord with all our hearts, how do you think Jesus feels?**

- **What can each of us do to work for the Lord?**

Say: **God wants us to work for him with all our hearts for many good reasons. Through our work, others will see God's glory, and they, too, may be encouraged to know him. Before you leave today, give your heart pin to someone who works at the church. Your pin will be a great way to make someone feel loved and encouraged!**

Pray: **Dear Lord, thank you for giving us worthwhile work to do for you. Thank you, also, for the work that people do so often in our church. We pray that our heart pins will encourage those people who serve you so well. In Jesus' name, amen.**

100 Percent Pure Heart

Bible Point

God can wipe away our sins.

Scripture

"Create in me a pure heart, O God, and renew a steadfast spirit within me" (Psalm 51:10).

Have you ever been really dirty? That's how we are before the Lord—really dirty. But he "scrubs" our hearts clean with his love and forgiveness, creating a new person. This craft will remind the children that God can make our hearts and lives new and clean. Your children will give these crafts to people who love them and know them well.

Supplies

- 1 small bar of soap per child (Ivory brand works best)
- 1 plastic knife per child
- newspaper
- toothpicks

Steps

1. Spread a piece of newspaper in front of each child. Give each child a bar of soap and a plastic knife. Direct kids to cut one end off the bar to make it a square shape. Then show them how to score a large heart shape on the soap with the knife.

2. Beginning at the corners, have kids use their knives to start carving away the soap to form the heart shape they scored on their bars.

3. When they have finished carving the heart, the children can scrape away the brand-name letters that remain on the soap. Have each child use a toothpick to carve a name of a family member to give this "clean" message to.

Closing

Discuss these questions with your children:

- **How do you feel when you've done something you know you shouldn't have?**

- **How is taking a bath and getting clean with soap like being forgiven for things we know we shouldn't have done?**

- **Why does God forgive us when we ask him to?**

Say: **God loves us so much that he's willing to forgive us for all the things we have done wrong. God wants to help us keep from doing those things again. Give your clean-heart soap to someone in your family who you know loves you. The heart soap will remind that person that God is always ready to help us have clean hearts.**

Pray: **Dear Jesus, thank you for loving us and forgiving our sins. Help us keep a pure heart so we can keep from sinning. We love you. Amen.**

A Gift for You

Bible Point

We should use the gifts God gave us to serve others.

Scripture

"Each one should use whatever gift he has received to serve others, faithfully administering God's grace in its various forms" (1 Peter 4:10).

God has given us gifts to worship and honor him. With these gift tags, families will have reminders to use their gifts faithfully to serve others and, ultimately, to serve God.

Supplies

- 1 plain manila file folder per child
- construction paper
- decorative scissors
- glue
- several 6-inch lengths of ribbon per child
- hole punch
- hole-reinforcement labels
- craft supplies, such as buttons, stickers, and beads
- markers and crayons

Steps

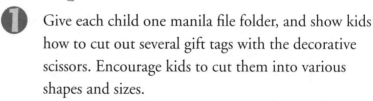

1. Give each child one manila file folder, and show kids how to cut out several gift tags with the decorative scissors. Encourage kids to cut them into various shapes and sizes.

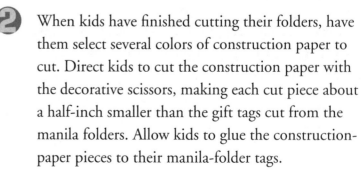

2. When kids have finished cutting their folders, have them select several colors of construction paper to cut. Direct kids to cut the construction paper with the decorative scissors, making each cut piece about a half-inch smaller than the gift tags cut from the manila folders. Allow kids to glue the construction-paper pieces to their manila-folder tags.

3 Encourage kids to decorate their gift tags with the craft supplies. Explain that they will not be writing names on their gift tags right now because the tags will be given to the person in each family who usually gives gifts—Mom, Dad, or Grandma, for example.

4 While kids are decorating their tags, punch a hole in the end of each tag. Help kids attach a hole-reinforcement label to the tag, string a piece of ribbon through the hole, and tie it off.

Closing

Discuss these questions with your children:

- **Why do we give gifts to others?**

- **What do you think are some of the special gifts God has given you?**

- **How can you use your gifts to help others know Jesus?**

Say: **The Bible says, "Each one should use whatever gift he has received to serve others, faithfully administering God's grace in its various forms" (1 Peter 4:10). When we use the gifts God gives us, we can honor God and help others have a friendship with Jesus. Put your gift tags with the gift-wrapping supplies at home. The next time someone in your family wraps a gift, it'll be a reminder that God has given his children gifts to help serve others.**

Pray: **God, thank you for giving us special gifts to serve you. Please help us use our gifts to help others know you. In Jesus' name, amen.**

Box of Deeds

Bible Point

God will help us show love to others and do good deeds.

Scripture

"And let us consider how we may spur one another on toward love and good deeds" (Hebrews 10:24).

We love to feel loved and be on the receiving end of a good deed. Your kids will love this treasure chest full of creative ideas for showing love and doing good deeds!

Supplies

- 1 small paper jewelry box per child
- glue
- assorted bright-colored puffy paints
- fine-tipped colored markers
- plastic jewels
- 1 piece of colored paper per child
- safety scissors

Tip

For a little extra "wow," use simple cardboard craft treasure chests. You can find these at most craft stores for a low cost.

Steps

1. Give each child a small paper jewelry box, and instruct kids to write "Good Deeds" on the lids with puffy paint.

2. Have kids decorate their boxes with markers and plastic jewels.

3. Direct kids to cut small strips of paper and write one simple, specific way to show love and kindness on each strip. Here are some examples:

- Give someone a hug.

- Do a chore for a family member without being asked.

- Give a parent or friend a flower.

- Tell someone Jesus loves him or her.

- Make a card for someone.

- Really listen to someone when he or she talks to you.

- Tell a friend what you like about him or her.

 Allow kids to place their ideas inside their treasure boxes.

Closing

Discuss these questions with your children:

- **What are some ways you can show someone love?**

- **When was it hard for you to do a good deed for someone else?**

- **Why does God want us to do good for others?**

Say: **"And let us consider how we may spur one another on toward love and good deeds" (Hebrews 10:24). God wants us to love others and do good things for them, but this passage says we should also encourage one another to do the same. Your treasure chests will be good reminders for your family members to do good things for each other.**

Pray: **Dear Lord, thank you for showing us how to love others. Please help us spur each other on toward love and good deeds every day. In Jesus' name, amen.**

Calling God

Bible Point

We can call on God for anything.

Scripture

"Give thanks to the Lord, call on his name" (1 Chronicles 16:8a).

Cell phones are nearly everywhere, which shows how much we value communication. God loves communicating with us too! He desires our thanksgiving and praises, and he wants us to call on him in our good times and bad. The children will use this craft to remind their families to "phone God"—to call on him often through prayer.

Supplies

- 1 sheet of poster board for every four kids
- hole-reinforcement labels
- crayons or markers
- adhesive magnetic strips
- 1 pair of sharp scissors for leader
- Bible

Before Craft

Cut the poster board into one cell phone shape for each child.

Steps

1. Give each child twelve hole-reinforcement labels, and direct kids to put the labels on the proper places on the keypad of the cell phone to represent the buttons for 1 through 9, 0, and the symbols "*" and "#."

2. Help the children write the words of 1 Chronicles 16:8a and "Call on God today" on the screen of each phone above the number pad. Have kids write in numbers and symbols on the key pad.

3. Use sharp scissors to cut two pieces of adhesive magnetic strip for each child, and instruct kids to attach them to the back of their cell phones.

Closing

Discuss these questions with your children:

- **What does it mean to "call on God"?**

- **When do you call on God?**

- **How can you remind others to talk to God through prayer?**

Say: **God loves it when we talk to him. He wants us to share everything with him: our happy times as well as our sad or troubled times. We can talk to God at any time for any reason. Share your craft with a family member. Ask that person to stick the phone on the refrigerator or somewhere else where it will remind him or her to "call" on God.**

Pray: **Dear God, it is so awesome that a mighty God like you is available anytime to talk to us—you even *desire* to have a conversation with your children! Help us remember that we can call on you at any time, for any reason. In Jesus' name, amen.**

Furry Faith Friends

Bible Point

Always be ready to share your faith with others.

Scripture

"Preach the Word; be prepared in season and out of season" (2 Timothy 4:2a).

It's not always easy to share our faith with others. But God wants every person on earth to hear about his love. And he wants *us* to do the talking! With this craft, children will help someone remember, in a fun way, to always be ready to share the good news of Jesus Christ.

Supplies

- yarn

- one 3-inch square of heavy cardboard or a 3½-inch floppy disk per child

- sharp scissors for leader's use only

- 1 egg-carton section per child

- 1 pair of wiggle eyes per child

- chenille wire

- 1 photocopy of the hand and Bible shown in the margin per child

- glue

- safety scissors

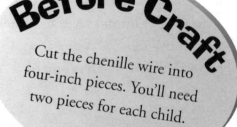

Before Craft

Cut the chenille wire into four-inch pieces. You'll need two pieces for each child.

Steps

1. Have each child wrap yarn around a piece of cardboard about one hundred times or more in one direction.

2. Help each child slip a six-inch piece of yarn under the wrapped yarn at one edge of the cardboard and tie a tight knot in it. Then cut through the yarn at the other edge.

3 Have kids glue the knot of the pompom to the top of an inverted egg-carton section and spread out the strands evenly to cover the carton section.

4 Help kids glue on wiggle eyes and poke chenille wires into the egg section for arms.

5 Have each child cut out the hand picture from the photocopy and glue it onto one of the arms. Then have each child cut out the Bible picture, fold it in half, and glue it onto the other arm.

Closing

Discuss these questions with your children:

• **When have you told someone about Jesus?**

• **What was the person's reaction?**

• **How can we always be ready to "preach the Word," or tell others about Jesus?**

Say: **We serve a God who is good, loving, and great. He loves everyone so much and wants to have a friendship with everyone. That's why God wants us to share our faith with others. Plan on giving your Furry Faith Friend to a Christian family member so that person can remember to tell others about Jesus too. It'll give your family member a playful nudge to share about faith, and it will make him or her smile. And *you'll* be spreading the Word too!**

Pray: **Jesus, you are a great God. It is a privilege for us to be able to share you with others. Help us this week, Lord, to be ready to share our faith. Amen.**

Grace Place Mat

Bible Point

God's free gift of salvation is placed before us.

Scripture

"For it is by grace you have been saved, through faith—and this not from yourselves, it is the gift of God—not by works, so that no one can boast" (Ephesians 2:8-9).

God has a wonderful gift to give us through his love for us. We can't pay for the gift, and we can't earn it. It's the gift of forgiveness, and it comes to us when we believe in God's Son, Jesus. Each child will share the message of Jesus by creating and giving this Grace Place Mat to someone who needs to receive God's free gift of salvation.

Supplies

- 1 clear plastic report cover with no binder holes per child
- one 20-inch length of ¹/₂-inch ribbon per child
- one 8¹/₂x11-inch piece of card stock per child
- markers or crayons
- one 8¹/₂x11-inch piece of printed fabric per child
- one 3x5-inch piece of solid fabric per child
- fabric scissors
- double-sided tape
- ruler
- Bibles

Before Craft

Cut each 3x5-inch piece of solid fabric into a cross shape. You'll need one cross for each child.

Steps

 Have the children read the words of Ephesians 2:8-9. Help young readers if needed. Set out markers or crayons, and ask the children to each write the verse neatly on one side of an 8¹/₂x11-inch piece of card stock.

2 Give each child an 8½x11-inch piece of fabric, and have the children tape the fabric and the card stock back to back, allowing the words of the verse to show.

3 Direct each child to use a ruler to measure and cut an 11-inch and an 8½-inch piece of ribbon. Show the children how to form a "t" with the ribbon, then have them tape the ribbon to the fabric to make the place mat look like the top of a gift.

4 Give each child a 3x5-inch cloth cross. Instruct kids to tape the crosses onto the front of their fabric pieces wherever they think looks best.

5 Give each child a plastic report cover to protect his or her place mat.

Closing

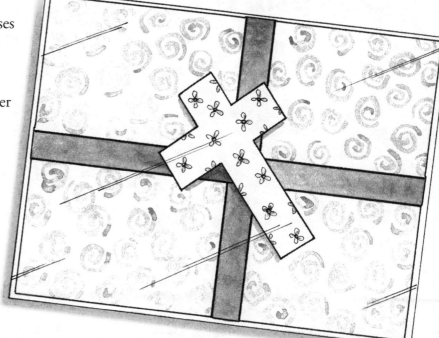

Discuss these questions with your children:

- **In what ways does your place mat remind you of a gift?**

- **What gift has God given us? Why?**

- **How can you share that gift with someone else?**

Say: **Gifts come in all shapes and sizes, but God's gift is the biggest and best of all. He wants us to accept his gift of forgiveness through Jesus. Give your place mat to a family member as a gift, and tell that person about God's best gift.**

Pray: **Dear Lord, thank you for giving us your Son. Please help us share your gift of forgiveness with others. In Jesus' name, amen.**

Let Love Inside!

Bible Point

God helps us learn to love.

Scripture

"Love is patient, love is kind. It does not envy, it does not boast, it is not proud. It is not rude, it is not self-seeking, it is not easily angered, it keeps no record of wrongs" (1 Corinthians 13:4-5).

Growing in Christ means learning to love. Children will discover the qualities of genuine love and, with God's help, begin to demonstrate those qualities in their homes. Family members will have a visual reminder to "let love inside" their hearts and homes each time they see this child-crafted door hanger.

Supplies

- one 1½-inch craft foam heart per child
- colored card stock
- construction paper
- confetti with hearts, "love," or similar theme
- glue sticks
- 1 hole punch for every three children
- two 4-foot pieces of different-colored yarn per child
- fine-tipped markers or pens
- Bibles

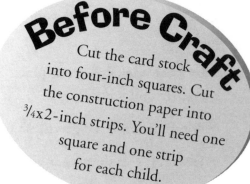

Before Craft Cut the card stock into four-inch squares. Cut the construction paper into ¾x2-inch strips. You'll need one square and one strip for each child.

Steps

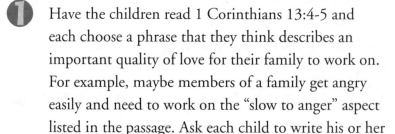

1 Have the children read 1 Corinthians 13:4-5 and each choose a phrase that they think describes an important quality of love for their family to work on. For example, maybe members of a family get angry easily and need to work on the "slow to anger" aspect listed in the passage. Ask each child to write his or her phrase on a foam heart.

2 Show kids how to accordion-fold the construction paper into thirds. Have them glue one end to the back of the heart and the other to the center of the square so the heart pops up slightly. Next, have kids glue confetti onto the square surrounding the heart.

3 Have kids punch three evenly spaced holes in all sides of the square except one. The edge without holes is the top.

4 Show kids how to lay their two pieces of yarn together and begin weaving the yarn through the holes, with the middle of the lengths of yarn positioned at the center bottom hole.

5 Have kids tie the loose ends into a bow, forming a loop to suspend the hanger from a doorknob.

Closing

Discuss these questions with your children:

- **What qualities of love do you notice in your family?**

- **How does your family show patience and kindness?**

- **In what ways does God help our families learn more about love?**

Say: **God planned for people in families to love each other. But often we are not patient or kind like God is. God forgives us and helps us learn to love. When you or your family members see this craft hanging on your door, remember what God's love is like and ask him to help your family let love inside.**

Pray: **Dear God, thank you for showing us what real love is like. Help our families grow in love for you and for each other. In Jesus' name, amen.**

Little Greetings

Bible Point

We can honor God by loving others.

Scripture

"Be devoted to one another in brotherly love. Honor one another above yourselves" (Romans 12:10).

Parents in your church will be surprised when they open their babies' diaper bags—and find loving cards from their babies!

Supplies

- colorful construction paper
- 1 envelope per child
- safety scissors
- stapler
- markers
- ruler

Steps

1. Hand out one envelope to each child, and tell kids to each select, fold, and trim a piece of construction paper to make a card that fits inside the envelope.

2. Explain to kids that they will make cards for parents in the church, but the cards will be from the parents' babies and toddlers! Direct each child to write a phrase, such as one of the following ideas, on the front of his or her card.

   - Thank you for caring for me!
   - I'm so happy to be in such a caring family!
   - Thank you for loving me!
   - You're such a blessing to me!

3. Tell kids to each cut out a heart shape that will fit on the inside of the card. Have kids write "I love you!" on the hearts.

4 Help kids each cut out a ¹/₂x6-inch strip of paper, and show them how to fold the strips to make accordion-style springs.

5 Show kids how to staple one end of the spring to the card and glue the other end to the back of the heart shape. Allow time for the kids to complete this step.

6 Tell kids to decorate their cards and envelopes with markers.

Closing

Discuss these questions with your children:

- **How do people show their love for each other?**

- **Who does Jesus want us to love?**

- **Why does Jesus want us to love others?**

- **How can we show our love to others?**

Say: **Everyone enjoys feeling honored and loved. God wants us to put others first, even before ourselves. People who take care of young children don't always get to feel honored or put first because they are so busy sharing their love and putting the young children first. Your homemade greeting cards will help the babies' families feel very appreciated and loved.**

Take the cards to the nursery or preschool, and ask workers to hide them in diaper bags or cribs so family members see them when they return for their children.

Pray: **Dear Lord, thank you for loving us. Help us love others as you have loved us. We pray that other families feel loved and appreciated with our cards today. In Jesus' name, amen.**

Perseverance Prizes

Bible Point

Facing a hard time is a chance to grow in faith.

Scripture

"Consider it pure joy, my brothers, whenever you face trials of many kinds, because you know that the testing of your faith develops perseverance" (James 1:2-3).

Children and their families face trials—more than you may imagine. Ask your kids to give this craft to family members as an encouragement to trust God through tough issues because God uses those issues to strengthen our faith.

Supplies

- 1 juice-can lid per child (smooth aluminum lids from cardboard containers)
- 1-foot length of 1-inch-wide heavyweight blue or red ribbon per child
- aluminum foil
- paper clips
- tacky glue

Steps

1 Give each child a six-inch length of aluminum foil and a juice-can lid. Have the children wrap the foil around the lids.

2 Prompt the children to think of something that has been hard to go through for their families: loss of a job, money issues, or a divorce, for example. Give each child a paper clip, and instruct the children to use a bent end of the clip to etch pictures in the foil that represent their hard times. For example, they could etch a broken heart or sad face.

3 Ask kids to place their "medals" facedown in front of them and to each choose a piece of ribbon. Help each child tie the ribbon into a loop with a knot.

 Show kids how to attach the ribbon to the medal by applying a dot of tacky glue to the top of the medal and pressing the ribbon firmly onto the glue. Have them pinch the lids and ribbons together between their fingers until they dry.

Closing

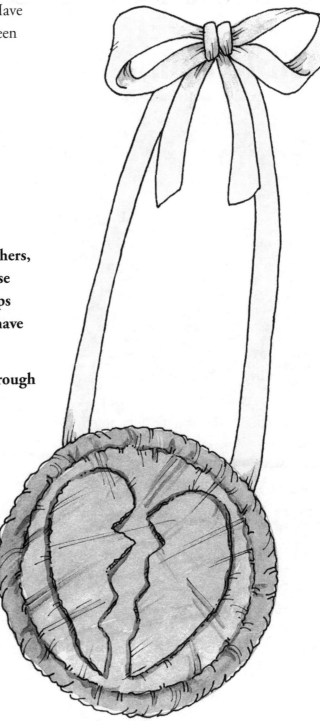

Discuss these questions with your children:

- **What is an award you've won?**

- **What did you have to do to win that prize?**

- **The Bible says, "Consider it pure joy, my brothers, whenever you face trials of many kinds, because you know that the testing of your faith develops perseverance" (James 1:2-3). Why should we have joy when we face hard times or challenges?**

- **What kind of "prize" can we earn by going through hard, challenging times?**

Say: **Sometimes God allows us to go through hard times. God knows that when we face hard times, we can grow in our trust for him. That's a great prize! When you get home, give your medal to someone in your family who is struggling with a tough situation right now. Explain how facing a hard time is an opportunity to win a valuable prize.**

Pray: **God, thank you for being with us even in hard times. Help us always trust and obey you so we can grow stronger in our faith. We love you, Lord. In Jesus' name, amen.**

"Thumb-body Cares" Pillow Treat

Bible Point

Jesus cares when we are worried.

Scripture

"So do not worry, saying, 'What shall we eat?' or 'What shall we drink?' or 'What shall we wear?'…But seek first his kingdom and his righteousness, and all these things will be given to you as well" (Matthew 6:31, 33).

Our lives are filled with stress and, often, worry. Jesus understands, and he's promised that once he's first in our lives, everything else will gradually fall into place! This treat will be a sweet reminder for a family member to focus first on Jesus.

Supplies

- one 6-inch square of soft fabric per child
- 1 unusable CD
- safety scissors
- 3 to 4 chocolate candies per child
- one 7-inch piece of yarn per child
- 1 index card per child
- hole punch
- 1 stamp pad for every 10 children
- fabric pen
- Bible

Before Craft

Use the fabric pen and the CD to trace a circle onto each piece of fabric.

Steps

1. Give each child a piece of fabric, and have kids cut out the circles.

2. Show children how to fold the index cards in half and write "Thumb-body Cares" on the outside. Help kids write the words of Matthew 6:31, 33 on the inside of the cards.

3 Direct each child to press a thumb on the stamp pad and to carefully apply a thumbprint to the front of the card under the words "Thumb-body Cares."

4 Tell kids to place several pieces of candy in the center of each cloth circle. Show them how to pull the edges up and tie them together with yarn. Help each child punch a hole in the card by the corner of the folded edge and attach the card to the yarn.

Closing

Discuss these questions with your children:

- **What are some things you worry about?**

- **What should we do when we feel worried?**

- **What can you do to comfort someone who is worried?**

Say: **Everyone worries about things sometimes. But Jesus wants us to focus on him first. The verse you just wrote on your craft reminds us that when we focus on Jesus, we don't have to worry about other things because he cares. He will take care of us. You can remind your family members that Jesus cares and wants them to focus on him. Place your craft on the pillow of someone in your family to remind that person that "Thumb-body Cares."**

Pray: **Dear Jesus, thank you for your love and care. Help us to focus on you so we can have a strong relationship with you first. In your name, amen.**

"Awesome God" Collage

Bible Point

Knowing God helps us become wise.

Scripture

"The fear of the Lord is the beginning of wisdom, and knowledge of the Holy One is understanding" (Proverbs 9:10).

The way to true wisdom takes more than gaining knowledge and experience. It takes humbling ourselves before the one true, powerful God and his Son, Jesus Christ. With this craft, children will help someone remember that walking in "fear of the Lord" is the way to becoming wise.

Supplies

- one 8½x11-inch piece of card stock per child
- one 5-foot piece of yarn per child
- old magazines, especially nature and travel editions
- safety scissors
- hole punch
- markers
- glue
- Bible

Steps

1. Have kids find and cut out magazine pictures that illustrate God's power, such as mountain scenes, the ocean, flowers growing, storms, and so on.

2. While everyone is looking for magazine pictures, ask kids to take turns using the hole punch to punch holes at about three-fourths to one-inch intervals around the edges of their card stock.

3. Have kids write the words of Proverbs 9:10 or the Bible Point on their pieces of card stock. Then have kids glue the pictures to the card stock and decorate the collages with markers.

4. When the collage is finished, show kids how to thread the yarn through the holes. Starting at a corner, thread

the yarn up through the hole from the back, loop it over the side and behind the collage again, and bring the yarn up through the next hole. Continue around the perimeter of the poster, then tie yarn ends together.

Closing

Discuss these questions with your children:

- **How do your pictures show God's power?**

- **What other things can you think of that show God's power?**

- **"Fear of the Lord" means to have a deep respect for God and God's power. How does having a deep respect for God help us become wise?**

Say: **God doesn't want us to fear him in the same way we are afraid of evil people or dangerous situations. But he does want us to respect him and know that he is more powerful than anything or anyone. It's like saying we know there's someone stronger, smarter, and more powerful than we are. It reminds us to trust God for what we need.**

Ask: • **How could this craft encourage someone in life?**

Say: **Think of a friend to give your craft to, reminding him or her that fear, or respect, of the Lord helps us become wise.** Give kids time to think. **Let's pray for the people you thought about.**

Pray: **Dear Father, we praise you for being so powerful. And we thank you for your amazing love. Help us to encourage others this week to fear you and grow in wisdom. In Jesus' name, amen.**

Backpack Buttons

Bible Point

Wherever we go, God has good plans for us.

Scripture

" 'For I know the plans I have for you,' declares the Lord, 'plans to prosper you and not to harm you, plans to give you hope and a future' " (Jeremiah 29:11).

Thinking about the future can be a worrisome experience for kids. That's why they need to hear that God knows all about our unknown future. As your kids create this cool button craft for their friends to attach to their backpacks, it will help your kids (and their friends!) remember that our loving God is in control and has good plans for their future.

Supplies

- colored craft foam
- 1 large button per child (at least 1 inch in diameter)
- 1 chenille wire per child
- markers or pens
- hole punch

Before Craft

Cut the craft foam into 2¼-inch circles. You'll need one for each child.

Steps

1. Give each child a foam circle. Direct kids to write "Jeremiah 29:11" and "God has good plans for you!" around the circumference of the circle with markers or colorful pens.

2. Help each child punch two holes in the center of the foam circle about one-half inch apart.

3. Give each child a large button and a chenille wire. Show kids how to bend the chenille wire in half and insert the ends through the buttonholes and then through the holes in the circle. Kids will need to twist the chenille stems together two or three times to keep the button secure on the circle.

Closing

Discuss these questions with your children:

- **What are some of the things you carry in your backpack?**

- **Why do you carry a backpack?**

- **What are some things you are worried about?**

Say: **God tells us in Jeremiah 29:11 that he has good plans for us. The passage says, " 'For I know the plans I have for you,' declares the Lord, 'plans to prosper you and not to harm you, plans to give you hope and a future.' " You take your backpacks almost everywhere! God also goes with us everywhere, working out his great plan in our lives. We can trust God's plans because he loves us and knows what is best for us. Give your button to a friend this week to remind him or her that God has good plans for people who love him.**

Pray: **Dear God, thank you for having great plans for our future. Help us trust that your plan is best and encourage others to follow you too. In Jesus' name, amen.**

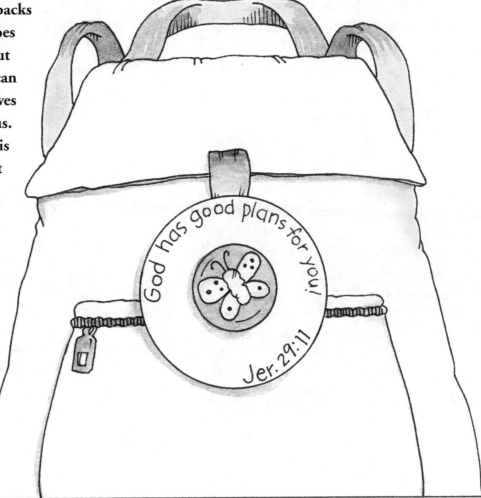

Come See His Glory

Bible Point

We can invite others to meet Jesus.

Scripture

"The Word became flesh and made his dwelling among us. We have seen his glory, the glory of the One and Only, who came from the Father, full of grace and truth" (John 1:14).

Most church visitors come because a friend or neighbor has invited them. At Christmas, neighbors without a church home may be especially receptive to an invitation from an enthusiastic child. This baby Jesus craft will provide children with an opportunity to reach out to others, inviting them to meet the Christ child.

Supplies

- one 4-inch doll pin per child
- fine-tipped black markers
- one 4-inch square of Christmas fabric per child
- 1-foot piece of yarn per child
- colored card stock
- markers or pens
- hole punch
- one 2x4-inch label per child, pre-printed with your church's name, address, and Christmas worship schedule

Before Craft

Cut the card stock so you have one 5x7-inch piece for each child.

Steps

1. Give each child a pre-printed label, and ask kids to affix their labels to their cards. Under the labels, have the children use pens to write the words to John 1:14 and to sign their first names.

2. Help each child punch a hole in the upper left corner of the card stock. Have each child thread the yarn through the hole and set the card and yarn aside.

 Lay a piece of fabric facedown in front of each child. Direct kids to each draw a face on the head of the doll pin with a fine-tipped marker and then position the pin diagonally on the fabric. Have kids gather the opposite corners of the fabric around the center of the doll pin like a blanket around a baby.

 Have kids help each other tie the yarn around the middle of the blanket in a bow, attaching the baby to the invitation. Secure the bow with a double knot.

Closing

Discuss these questions with your children:

- **Why is it such good news that Jesus came to earth?**

- **What are some ways we can help others know about Jesus?**

- **Who could you share this good news with?**

Say: **At Christmas, our church often has many new visitors. This is a wonderful time to invite friends or neighbors to come with you! Jesus coming to save us is good news that everyone should hear. Your family could bake cookies and take the cookies and your craft to a neighbor, inviting your neighbor to come to church with you!**

Pray: **Dear Jesus, thank you for coming to live with us and be our Savior. Help people who do not know you come to church this Christmas, and help them hear and believe the good news. In your name, amen.**

Come Worship With Us!
Carmel Lutheran Church
4850 East 31st Street
Christmas Eve 4pm, 6pm, 8pm & 10pm
Christmas Day - 10am

The Word became flesh and made his dwelling among us.
John 1:14

Impossible Opening

Bible Point

Nothing is impossible with God!

Scripture

"Nothing is impossible with God" (Luke 1:37).

Nothing is impossible for God! With this craft, children will encourage people by reminding them that God can do all things.

Supplies

- 1 piece of construction paper per child
- safety scissors
- crayons and markers

Steps

1. Give each child a piece of construction paper. Ask kids to decorate their papers and each write a note to a friend who is facing a tough challenge, such as a test or big game.

2. Tell kids that, even though it seems impossible, you'll show them how to walk through their pieces of paper. Ask for volunteers to try to figure out ways to "walk through" their notes.

3. After a few guesses, distribute a pair of safety scissors to each child. Show kids how to cut their papers according to the following directions.

4. Fold the paper in half, and cut off the entire fold *except* for about one-fourth inch at each end.

5. Starting at each remaining fold, cut across the width of the paper, stopping about one-fourth inch from the other end. You will make one cut from each fold.

6. Between the two cuts you made, alternate between the two sides of the folded paper, making similar cuts.

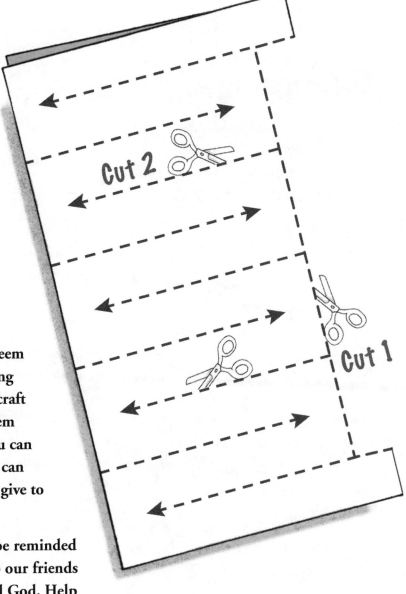

Each time, stop before you cut all the way through. Continue in an alternating pattern until you reach the end.

 Unfold your paper, and step through the not-so-impossible doorway you've created.

Closing

Discuss these questions with your children:

- **Think about a time you faced something that seemed impossible. How did God help you?**

- **What are some situations people you know are facing that might seem impossible for them?**

- **How can we encourage others when things seem impossible?**

Say: **Sometimes we need to do things that seem impossible for us to accomplish. But nothing is impossible for God! When you give this craft to a friend, talk about things in life that seem impossible. Then show your friend how you can walk through the impossible doorway. You can even show your friend how to make one to give to someone else!**

Pray: **Dear Jesus, you know who needs to be reminded about how big and powerful you are. Help our friends know that you are a mighty and wonderful God. Help all of us remember that nothing is impossible with you. Amen.**

Reflections of the Heart

Bible Point

Our hearts are what matter to God.

Scripture

"The Lord does not look at the things man looks at. Man looks at the outward appearance, but the Lord looks at the heart" (1 Samuel 16:7b).

Sometimes we think that if we looked different, we would be more popular or better people. This heart-shaped mirror will help your kids reflect on the fact that God values what is in our hearts more than how we look. Both the givers and recipients of this craft will be reminded to value others' hearts and not just see their outward appearances.

Supplies

- one 8½x11-inch piece of craft foam per child
- one 8½x11-inch piece of mirror paper per child
- pencils
- glue
- colored markers
- puffy paint
- safety scissors
- 1 paint stir stick per child
- small heart-shaped craft foam pieces

Steps

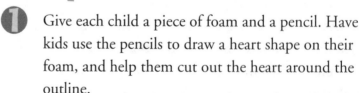 Give each child a piece of foam and a pencil. Have kids use the pencils to draw a heart shape on their foam, and help them cut out the heart around the outline.

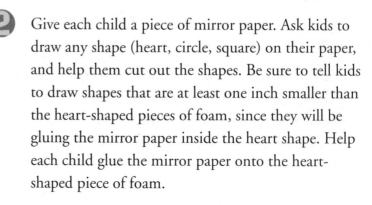 Give each child a piece of mirror paper. Ask kids to draw any shape (heart, circle, square) on their paper, and help them cut out the shapes. Be sure to tell kids to draw shapes that are at least one inch smaller than the heart-shaped pieces of foam, since they will be gluing the mirror paper inside the heart shape. Help each child glue the mirror paper onto the heart-shaped piece of foam.

Tell the children to use puffy paint to write "The Lord looks at the heart!" on the heart-shaped foam between the edge of the mirror paper and edge of the foam. Give kids craft supplies and small heart-shaped foam pieces to decorate their mirrors.

 Give kids paint stir sticks to decorate, and help them glue the sticks to the back of their foam hearts.

Closing

Discuss these questions with your children:

- **What do you like best about your friends?**

- **Why does God care more about who we are than the way we look?**

- **What kind of people does God want us to be?**

Say: **The Lord cares deeply about what is in our hearts. We can mirror his actions by also looking at what's in people's hearts, instead of just their outward appearance. As you give this mirror to a friend, tell that person what you like about him or her.**

Pray: **Dear Lord, we pray that you will help us notice what is in the hearts of our friends, instead of just seeing their outward appearances. And help us reflect your beauty and be a mirror image of you. In Jesus' name, amen.**

Right Yo-Yo

Bible Point

God wants us to do what is right.

Scripture

"Do not repay anyone evil for evil. Be careful to do what is right in the eyes of everybody" (Romans 12:17).

In his love, God has shown us mercy. His command is to reflect his mercy when we interact with others. This craft will be a reminder of how to act toward others, no matter how people treat us.

Supplies

- 1 blank index card per child
- craft foam
- one 3-foot piece of string per child
- 8 pennies per child
- brass fasteners
- stapler
- safety scissors
- markers
- mailing tape or duct tape

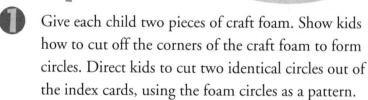

Before Craft

Cut the craft foam into two 2½-inch squares for each child.

Steps

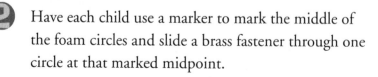

1. Give each child two pieces of craft foam. Show kids how to cut off the corners of the craft foam to form circles. Direct kids to cut two identical circles out of the index cards, using the foam circles as a pattern.

2. Have each child use a marker to mark the middle of the foam circles and slide a brass fastener through one circle at that marked midpoint.

3 Tell kids to tie one end of their string into a knot around the brass fastener ends. Then help kids tie a one-inch loop in the other end of the string. Show kids how to slide the fastener through the second foam circle at its midpoint and fold down the fastener ends tightly against the second circle.

4 Instruct kids to each tape four pennies flat to the face of one foam circle, keeping the pennies as close as possible without overlapping them. Have them repeat the process on the other side.

5 Help each child staple the two paper circles to the foam circles around the edges, using at least four staples each. Make sure any staple ends along the inside are pushed flat against the foam. Allow kids to decorate the yo-yos with markers.

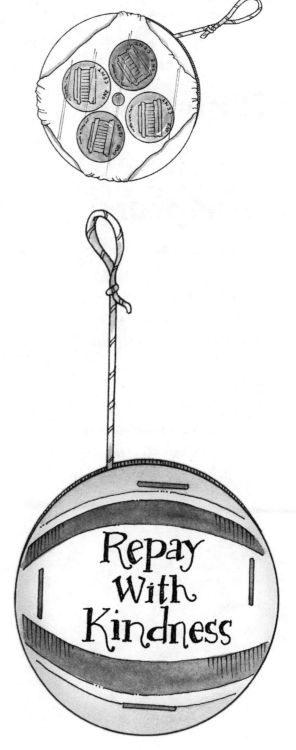

Closing

Discuss these questions with your children:

• **What's so special about yo-yos?**

• **How is the way we treat someone who is mean to us like a yo-yo?**

Say: **The Bible tells us that instead of being mean to people who are mean to us, we should treat those people with kindness. That means we should repay evil with goodness. That's a lot like a yo-yo because yo-yos bounce back. The yo-yos we made can help others remember to always bounce back with kindness.**

Pray: **God, thank you for showing us how to love. Help us have a loving attitude toward others, even when it's hard. In Jesus' name, amen.**

Trusty Sun Catchers

Bible Point

Trust in the Lord.

Scripture

"Trust in the Lord with all your heart and lean not on your own understanding; in all your ways acknowledge him, and he will make your paths straight" (Proverbs 3:5-6).

God wants us to trust him instead of leaning on our own understanding. As they turn in the breeze, these bright sun catchers will be reminders to turn to God in trust.

Supplies

- 1 blank CD per child
- 1 sheet of colored craft foam per child
- glue
- safety scissors
- 2 green chenille wires per child
- fine-tipped markers
- one 18-inch length of yarn per child

Steps

1 Help kids cut craft foam into flower petals about three inches long. Each child should cut at least five petals.

2 Give each child a CD. Tell kids to carefully use fine-tipped markers to write "Trust in the Lord—Proverbs 3:5-6" on the front of the CDs.

3 Show kids how to glue the foam petals around the outside edge of each CD.

4 Demonstrate how to loop a green chenille wire through the center of the CD and down the side and how to twist it to look like a stem. Let each child twist the other chenille wire around the stem to add leaves.

5 Help kids glue yarn to the top of their flowers for hanging.

Closing

Discuss these questions with your children:

- **When is it hard for you to trust God?**

- **Why is it such a good idea to trust God?**

- **How can we encourage each other to trust God even when it's hard?**

Say: **God knows everything about us. He knows what's good and bad for us, and he knows what's going to happen in the future. Plus, God loves us. So it only makes sense to trust in the Lord. Give your Trusty Sun Catcher to a friend to remind that person to trust God every day. When your friend sees the sun catcher turn in the breeze, he or she can remember to turn to God with trust.**

Pray: **Dear God, thank you for taking care of us. Help us trust you with all our hearts, and help us turn to you in every situation. In Jesus' name, amen.**

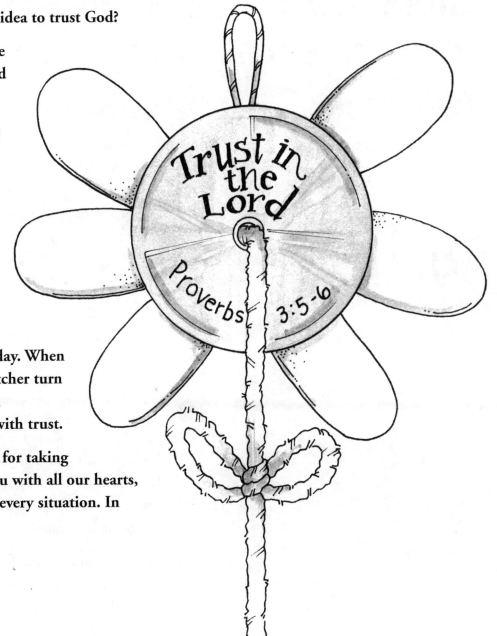

Wise Owls

Bible Point

God gives us wisdom.

Scripture

"If any of you lacks wisdom, he should ask God, who gives generously to all without finding fault, and it will be given to him" (James 1:5).

With this craft, children will encourage their friends and remind them that God gives wisdom to those who ask.

Supplies

- 1 piece of card stock per child
- crayons
- safety scissors
- 2 chenille wires per child
- tape
- 1 roll of Smarties candies per child

Steps

1 Give each child a piece of card stock. Instruct kids to each use the crayons to draw and color a large owl without legs on the piece of card stock. Use the illustration in the margin as a guide.

2 Ask the children to each think of someone they might give the owl to, such as a friend who will be taking a test, is working on a project, or is struggling in school. Have each child write a message on the owl for that person. For example, "I'm praying for God to give you the 'Smarties' while you take your test!"

3 After the children have finished decorating the owls, have them cut out their owls. While they're cutting, give each child two chenille wires.

4 Have kids tape their chenille wires to the backs of their owls to form legs hanging just below the bottom of the owls.

5 Give each child a roll of Smarties candies and show kids how to wrap the chenille wires around the Smarties to look like the owl is grasping the roll.

Closing

Say: **Owls are known as wise animals. People sometimes think wisdom is just being smart. But being smart for a test and being wise in life are two different things. When we have wisdom, we know the difference between right and wrong, and we know to do what's right.**

Ask: • **How can you gain wisdom from God?**

• **Why do you think God gives us wisdom to do what's right?**

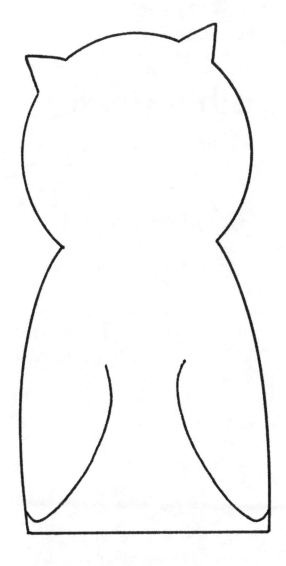

Say: **Sometimes it's hard to know the right thing to do. God can give us the wisdom we need in those times. Share your craft with the friend you've chosen who needs to be reminded that God gives us wisdom. It will also be an encouragement for his or her big test!**

Pray: **Dear God, thank you for promising to give us your wisdom when we ask you. Please give us wisdom to do the things you would have us do. In Jesus' name, amen.**

63

"Wonderful Words" Pen

Bible Point

God helps us keep our thoughts and words pure.

Scripture

"Finally, brothers, whatever is true, whatever is noble, whatever is right, whatever is pure, whatever is lovely, whatever is admirable—if anything is excellent or praiseworthy—think about such things" (Philippians 4:8).

The words we use, written or spoken, reflect what's in our hearts. The Bible tells us to be on guard and to think only of things that are good, pure, and holy. When we do this, our hearts are protected from things that shouldn't be there. As they make this craft, your children will consider the words that will be written with the pens. They will give the pens to friends, who can use them to write words that honor God.

Supplies

- 1 plain, nonretractable ball point pen per child
- assorted colors of polymer clay, 2 ounces per child
- baking sheet
- parchment paper
- oven

Before Craft

Preheat a nearby oven to 225 degrees.

Steps

1. Direct children to each form about fifty small, pea-sized balls of the polymer clay in different colors.

2. Give each child a pen. Have kids start covering their pens with the balls of clay and smoothing them out, creating a colorful outside layer. This does not need to be thick. Have kids cover the pen completely except for the writing tip.

3. Cover the bottom of the baking sheet with parchment paper. Ask kids to place their pens on the baking sheet and write their names beside their pens.

4. Bake the pens in the oven for about ten minutes. Let the pens cool completely before using.

Closing

Discuss these questions with your children:

- **How do you feel after you say or do something you know isn't pleasing to God?**

- **How can we keep ourselves from thinking about things that don't please God?**

- **What kinds of things should we be thinking about?**

Say: **Whether written or spoken, our words can be very powerful. They show the world what is in our hearts. By keeping our minds only on things that are pleasing to God, the words we say and write are more likely to be words that are good. When you give this pen to a friend, tell him or her that it is for writing encouraging words to family members and other friends, words that are pleasing to God and show that his or her heart is pure.**

Pray: **Dear Jesus, help us keep our minds on things that are pleasing to you. Help us remember that what is in our hearts comes out as our words. In your name, amen.**

Bubble Buddies

Bible Point

We can give God our worries.

Scripture

"Cast all your anxiety on him because he cares for you" (1 Peter 5:7).

Sometimes kids have grown-up-sized problems: where to get their next meal, where they'll sleep tonight, whether Dad will be in jail again next week, and the list goes on. Your children have an opportunity to reach out to these kids and help them know what to do with that endless list of worries. Use this craft to touch kids' lives.

Supplies

- $\frac{1}{3}$ cup of liquid dish detergent
- 5 cups of water
- $2\frac{1}{2}$ tablespoons of glycerin or white corn syrup
- 1 chenille wire per child
- 1 clean baby food jar with lid per child
- 1 mailing label per child
- 1 empty pitcher
- 1 large wooden spoon
- 1 measuring cup
- markers
- tape

Steps

1. Help the children mix the following bubble solution in a pitcher: $\frac{1}{3}$ cup of detergent, 5 cups of water, and $2\frac{1}{2}$ tablespoons of glycerin or white corn syrup.

2. Give each child a baby food jar. Have the children fill their jars with bubble solution and place the lids on the jars.

3. Give each child a mailing label and a marker. Help kids write "Jesus Cares for You—1 Peter 5:7" on their

labels. Encourage kids to decorate the labels and put them on the jars.

 Show kids how to bend a chenille wire into the shape of a bubble wand. Direct the children to tape their wands to the side of the jars.

Closing

Discuss these questions with your children:

- **How is blowing bubbles like "casting" our worries on God?**

- **What happens to our worries when we give them to God?**

Say: **Sometimes there are things that worry us. God wants us to tell him those things because he cares for us. There are children in our community who have a lot of worries and don't know they can give them to God. We're going to give our Bubble Buddies to a group of kids who need to hear about the love of Jesus.**

Give your crafts to a group home or foster-care agency in your area. If you have time, your children will benefit from going together to give these gifts.

Pray: **God, thank you for loving us and hearing our prayers. We praise you for your love, and we want to help others know you like we do. We love you. In Jesus' name, amen.**

Calendar of Strength

Bible Point

God gives us strength.

Scripture

"I can do everything through him who gives me strength" (Philippians 4:13).

With this craft, your children will help care for caregivers who may need to be reminded about where to turn for strength. No one can do God's work without God!

Supplies

- objects to use for rubbings, such as keys, stencils, die-cut shapes, and coins
- crayons
- 8½x11-inch copier paper, cut into fourths (you'll need two fourths for each child)
- hole punch
- poster board in four bright colors, cut into 5½x7-inch pieces (you'll need one per child)
- glue
- 1-foot chenille wire
- calendar to reference future days
- Bible

Steps

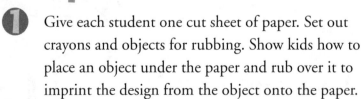 Give each student one cut sheet of paper. Set out crayons and objects for rubbing. Show kids how to place an object under the paper and rub over it to imprint the design from the object onto the paper.

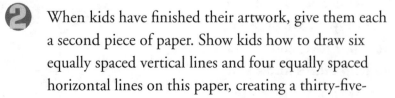 When kids have finished their artwork, give them each a second piece of paper. Show kids how to draw six equally spaced vertical lines and four equally spaced horizontal lines on this paper, creating a thirty-five-

square grid. Help kids label each grid with a month and use the calendar to number the days.

3 Open the spiral book, and help kids glue each picture onto a left page and each calendar month onto a right page. Write Philippians 4:13 on the front.

Closing

Discuss these questions with your children:

• **How do we deal with hard things?**

• **How can God help us when we have something hard to do?**

Say: **God promises to help us do anything he asks us to do. We're going to give our calendar to a place where people in need go for help. This can be a reminder to the people who work there that God can give them strength to help others.**

As a class, decide on a place to take your calendar: a homeless shelter, a pregnancy center, or a residential treatment center, for example.

Pray: **Lord, thank you for giving us strength. Help us remember that you love us and strengthen us in difficult times. In Jesus' name, amen.**

Before Craft

Punch five holes down one length of each piece of poster board, spaced about one inch apart. Stack the pieces of poster board together, and thread the chenille wire through the holes, creating a spiral booklet. Bend the ends of the chenille wire to secure them.

Comfort Cards

Bible Point

God will comfort us when we need him.

Scripture

"Come to me, all you who are weary and burdened, and I will give you rest" (Matthew 11:28).

Jesus tells us that if we take our problems to him, he will comfort us and give us the rest we need. With this craft, your children will help people remember that Jesus is a refuge when things get tough.

Supplies

- one 9x12-inch piece of felt per child
- cotton or foam pillow stuffing
- assorted craft foam shapes
- fabric scissors
- craft items, such as buttons and beads
- fabric glue
- construction paper
- markers
- stapler

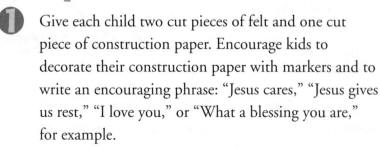

Before Craft

Cut each piece of felt in half, creating two 6x9-inch pieces for each child. Cut the construction paper into fourths. You'll need one fourth for each child.

Steps

1 Give each child two cut pieces of felt and one cut piece of construction paper. Encourage kids to decorate their construction paper with markers and to write an encouraging phrase: "Jesus cares," "Jesus gives us rest," "I love you," or "What a blessing you are," for example.

2 Set out assorted craft-foam shapes and craft items, such as buttons and beads. Have each child use the fabric glue to attach the construction paper to a piece of felt. Encourage kids to decorate around the construction paper by gluing foam shapes and craft items onto the felt.

3 While the glue dries, help kids carefully lay the two pieces of felt back to back and staple three sides together.

4 Set out the pillow stuffing, and show kids how to gently stuff the pillows until soft. Help them staple the final side, closing the hole.

Closing

Discuss these questions with your children:

- **When have you needed comfort from someone?**

- **What are some ways you've comforted others?**

- **How can Jesus use you to comfort someone else?**

Say: **Sometimes people have a hard day, and they need to take some time to rest. Jesus promised to help us when we're having a hard time because he loves us. Take your craft to someone who needs to feel comforted in a hard time.**

Pray: **Dear Jesus, thank you for loving us enough to comfort each one of us when we need rest. Help us find chances to share your comfort with others. Amen.**

Get Strong

Bible Point

We can be strong in difficult times.

Scripture

"Be strong and courageous. Do not be terrified; do not be discouraged, for the Lord your God will be with you wherever you go" (Joshua 1:9b).

God knows when we're having difficult times. God wants us to be strong and courageous during those times, relying on his strength when our own is not sufficient. By making and giving away edible weights, your children will remind people in need to be strong during troubling times.

Supplies

- 2 pretzel sticks per child
- 4 marshmallows per child
- 1 resealable bag per child
- markers
- stickers
- Bible

Steps

1. Give each child two pretzel sticks and four marshmallows.

2. Show children how to make barbells by pressing one marshmallow onto each end of the pretzel sticks, using a gentle twisting motion to insert the sticks.

3. Encourage kids to be creative as they decorate the resealable bags with markers and stickers. Help them write the words of Joshua 1:9b on their bags.

4. Have children place the weights in their decorated bags to give to people this week.

Closing

Discuss these questions with your children:

- **What is one time you were in a difficult situation?**

- **How were you strong and courageous during that time?**

- **How can Jesus help you be brave?**

Say: **Sometimes we don't feel very strong and brave during difficult times. God wants to help us be brave and courageous when we don't feel very strong by ourselves. We're going to give our barbells to people who need to know that Jesus can help them be strong, even though things aren't going the way they'd like.**

As a class, brainstorm people you can give these friendly reminders to. Some examples could be people in the hospital, families who have lost loved ones, or individuals who have lost jobs. If you have time, deliver the crafts as a group.

Pray: **Dear God, you are so mighty and strong. Thank you for helping us be strong in our lives. Help us encourage others with your strength too. In Jesus' name, amen.**

Hanging Hearts

Bible Point

Nothing can separate us from God's love.

Scripture

"For I am convinced that neither death nor life, neither angels nor demons, neither the present nor the future, nor any powers, neither height nor depth, nor anything else in all creation, will be able to separate us from the love of God that is in Christ Jesus our Lord" (Romans 8:38-39).

With this craft, children will encourage people to have faith in God's loving presence, no matter what the circumstances.

Supplies

- red craft foam
- stapler
- markers
- one 16-inch piece of craft cord or yarn per child

Before Craft

Before you begin the craft, cut the red craft foam into 8½-inch and 6-inch strips that are ¾ inch wide. You'll need two of each length for each child.

Steps

1. Give kids their strips of foam. Tell them to each stack their four strips together, with one of the short strips on the top, the other on the bottom, and the two long ones in between.

2. Have each child line up one set of the ends so they're even and staple them together about ½-inch from the edge. Then have each child turn the stack over and staple it from the other side at the same point.

staple →

3 With the unstapled ends of each stack pointing up, have kids bend the two left strips down to the left and the two right strips down to the right. Tell kids to join all four ends, line them up evenly, and staple the ends together from both sides.

4 Help kids attach a craft cord to the top of each heart, tying it in place.

5 Encourage kids to think of people in the hospital who need to be cheered up, and ask them to each write a person's name inside the small heart and Jesus' name on the inside of the large heart.

Closing

Discuss these questions with your children:

- **When have you been scared, lonely, or hurting?**

- **How does it make you feel to know that nothing can separate you from Jesus' love, no matter how you feel?**

- **What are some ways you can tell others about Jesus' love?**

Say: **We all face times we're afraid, lonely, or sick. But when we feel yucky, we can remember that *nothing* can separate us from God's love! He is always there with us, no matter what.**

Pray: **Father, thank you so much that there is no one and nothing in this world that can keep us away from you! Help us find just the right people to give these crafts to and help them know how much you love them. In Jesus' name, amen.**

Tip

Talk to a church office worker before your meeting time to collect names of church members who are in the hospital.

staple

"In My Heart" Puzzle

Bible Point

Love Jesus first.

Scripture

"But in your hearts set apart Christ as Lord. Always be prepared to give an answer to everyone who asks you to give the reason for the hope that you have" (1 Peter 3:15a).

Sometimes it's hard to make Jesus first in our hearts. And it can be just as difficult to tell others why we have hope in Jesus. This puzzle craft is an outreach opportunity for children to share their faith one little piece at a time.

Supplies

- 1 piece of card stock per child
- washable markers
- stickers of animals, food, or people
- safety scissors
- 1 colored lunch bag per child
- paper towels
- bowl of water
- Bible

Steps

1. Give each child a piece of card stock. Have each child cut a large heart out of the card stock.

2. Set out washable markers, and ask kids to color a cross in the center of each heart. Instruct kids to surround the crosses with stickers of things they love. Show them *immediately* how to dampen paper towels and quickly dab over their pictures to resemble a marbleized watercolor picture.

3. Direct kids to flip their hearts over. Help each child write the words of 1 Peter 3:15a and a brief personal message to the recipient, telling him or her why Jesus gives us hope.

 4 Give each child a colored lunch bag. Instruct kids to cut their hearts into ten or twelve puzzle-shaped pieces and place them in the bags.

Closing

Read the Bible verse to the children in your class, then discuss these questions with them:

- **Why should we make sure Jesus is first in our lives?**

- **Why should we tell others about Jesus?**

- **What are some ways we can share Jesus with others?**

Say: **When we love Jesus, he gives us a new hope for life. That's because Jesus offers us a wonderful gift of *eternal* life! Some people may be sad, sick, or lonely. They need to know the hope of Jesus. When you share your craft, tell the person who receives it about your hope and why you choose to love Jesus.**

Pray: **Jesus, thank you for being our hope in this world. Help us reach out to others and share our hope with them. In your name, amen.**

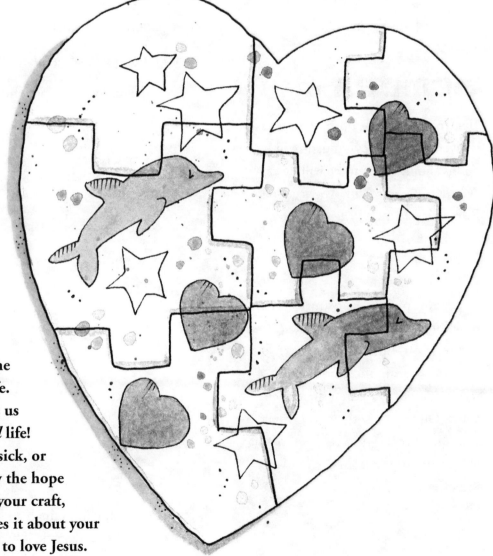

"It's a Boy!" Bookmarks

Bible Point

God sent Jesus for us.

Scripture

"For to us a child is born, to us a son is given, and the government will be on his shoulders. And he will be called Wonderful Counselor, Mighty God, Everlasting Father, Prince of Peace" (Isaiah 9:6).

For most people, Christmas is a time for celebrating with friends and relatives. But some people feel forgotten during the Christmas season. As your children share their crafts, God will use them to bring a message of comfort to those who long for reassurance that they've not been forgotten.

Supplies

- colored card stock
- 1-foot piece of $1/8$-inch-wide satin ribbon per child
- 1 decorative bead per child
- old Christmas cards
- safety scissors
- glue sticks
- colorful pens or markers
- hole punch
- Bible

Before Craft

Cut the card stock into one $3^1/2$x$8^1/2$-inch strip for each child.

Steps

1 Help each child punch a hole in the middle of one end of the card stock. Then help kids write the words of Isaiah 9:6 on one side of the bookmarks and sign their first names.

2 Encourage the children to look through old Christmas cards and choose pictures, borders, and words to cut out and use to decorate their bookmarks.

3 When they have cut out enough pictures and phrases for their bookmarks, have kids glue the pictures collage-style to the other side of their bookmarks.

4 Show kids how to make beaded tassels for the top of the bookmarks. Fold each ribbon in half, and insert the folded end through the hole from the back. Bring the loose ends of the ribbon over the top, thread them through the loop at the front of the bookmark, and pull snug. Thread the bead onto the ribbon, and tie a double knot so the bead cannot slip off.

Closing

Discuss these questions with your children:

- **Why do we celebrate Christmas?**

- **Why might a person feel lonely or sad at Christmas?**

- **How could remembering that God sent Jesus for us bring comfort?**

- **What might you say to help someone remember how much God loves him or her?**

Say: **Some people feel especially lonely or sad at Christmas. We can help those people remember that they're very special to God—he loves them so much that he sent his own Son to love them. Take your craft to someone who needs to be reminded that God sent Jesus for us.**

Pray: **Dear God, thank you for sending Jesus for us. Help us notice others who feel lonely or left out and remind them how much you love them. In Jesus' name, amen.**

Mail Center

Bible Point

God is abounding in love.

Scripture

"But you are a forgiving God, gracious and compassionate, slow to anger and abounding in love" (Nehemiah 9:17b).

With this craft, each child will provide a shut-in with a practical Mail Center—one with an eternal message! Each time the recipients of these crafts write to friends or family members, they can be reminded that God loves them!

Supplies

- 1 clean, empty container per child (an oatmeal box, unused deli container, recipe box, pencil box, or empty tissue box would work well)

- self-adhesive paper

- safety scissors

- markers

- decorating supplies, such as glitter glue and stickers

- 3 or 4 pens and pencils per child

- 4 or 5 pieces of writing paper per child

- 2 or 3 first-class letter stamps per child

Steps

1. Give each child a clean, empty container to decorate. Help kids wrap the containers in self-adhesive paper.

2. Help kids write the words of Nehemiah 9:17b on their containers. Then let them decorate the containers with glitter glue, stickers, ribbon, or paper cutouts—encourage kids to get creative!

3. Have kids tuck a few pencils, pens, sheets of inexpensive writing paper, and stamps into their containers.

Closing

Discuss these questions with your children:

- **How can this craft help someone experience God's love?**

- **When do you need to feel loved by someone?**

- **Why do you think God loves us so much?**

Say: **We'll deliver these crafts to people who might feel lonely sometimes. This craft can help those people communicate with friends and family members so they don't feel as lonely anymore. God communicates his love to us all the time, and it's good for us to share that love with others.**

Pray: **Dear God, thank you for your love. We know you have compassion for everyone, and we need to help others experience that compassion. Help us show your love to others this week. In Jesus' name, amen.**

Prayer Bracelets

Bible Point

Ask God for everything you need.

Scripture

"So I say to you: Ask and it will be given to you; seek and you will find; knock and the door will be opened to you" (Luke 11:9).

God wants to be generous with us. Jesus tells us to ask, seek, and knock. With this craft, children will help people remember to ask God for anything and trust him with everything.

Supplies

- craft foam
- pens or fine-tipped markers
- stapler
- two 1-foot lengths of yarn per child

Before Craft

Cut the craft foam into $\frac{1}{4}$x8-inch strips. You'll need three for each child.

Steps

1. Give each child three strips of foam. Tell them to each write the word "ASK" repeatedly across one of the foam strips, separating each word with a dot or a small heart, so that the strip is filled with the word. Have each child do the same with the other two strips, writing "SEEK" and "KNOCK" on them.

2. Have kids stack the three strips on top of one another, word sides up. Help them staple one end of each stack together.

3. Have kids choose partners, and show them how to braid the three strips together. One partner should hold the stapled end steady while the other braids.

Instruct kids to keep the word sides facing up as they braid (don't twist them).

4 Be ready to staple the other end as kids finish with their braids.

5 Have kids wind yarn around each end of the bracelets and tie it off tightly. The yarn will cover up the staples and make the ties for the bracelets. Cut off the excess ends.

Closing

Discuss these questions with your children:

- **What is one thing you have worried about in the past week?**

- **What is something you asked Jesus for this week?**

- **Jesus wants us to go to him with problems and things we worry about. How can you encourage others to pray about all their needs?**

Say: **The Bible says, "So I say to you: Ask and it will be given to you; seek and you will find; knock and the door will be opened to you" (Luke 11:9). This verse tells us to ask God to provide for us. We braided these prayer bracelets to remind people to ask God for help when they have problems or needs. Think of someone who needs to remember that God provides for us, and give this bracelet to that person today.**

Pray: **Dear Jesus, thank you for your friendship and for meeting our needs! Please help us remember to come to you when we're worried. We know you love to help out! In your name, amen.**

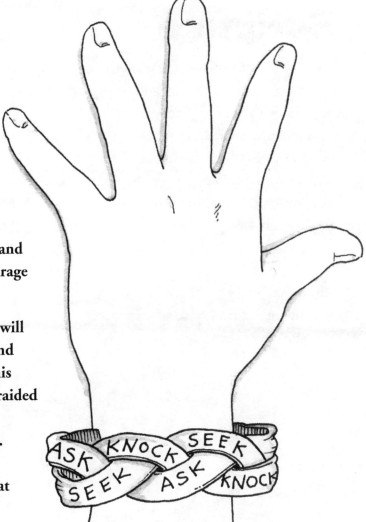

Protected With Peace

Bible Point

God guards our hearts with peace.

Scripture

"Do not be anxious about anything, but in everything, by prayer and petition, with thanksgiving, present your requests to God. And the peace of God, which transcends all understanding, will guard your hearts and your minds in Christ Jesus" (Philippians 4:6-7).

Your kids will give these pieces of art to children in the hospital to help those young patients remember to trust God.

Supplies

- wax paper
- construction paper
- safety scissors
- old crayons
- iron
- ironing board
- pencil sharpeners
- paper towels
- Bible

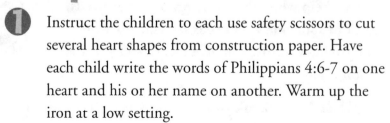

Tip

If you can't bring an ironing board, lay an old towel on a sturdy countertop.

Steps

1. Instruct the children to each use safety scissors to cut several heart shapes from construction paper. Have each child write the words of Philippians 4:6-7 on one heart and his or her name on another. Warm up the iron at a low setting.

2. Instruct the children to shave a few crayons with the pencil sharpeners.

3 Give each child two pieces of wax paper. Have each child arrange the heart shapes and crayon shavings on one sheet of wax paper and place the second sheet of wax paper on top of his or her work.

4 Ask kids to carefully set their work on the ironing board, staying clear of the hot iron. Place paper towels over the wax paper, and rub the iron over the paper towels until the two pieces of wax paper fuse together. This will take only a few seconds.

5 Set the children's work aside to cool down.

Closing

Say: **The Bible says that instead of worrying, we should tell God about situations that make us nervous. Then God can protect our hearts with his perfect peace. We'll give our heart pictures to children who are in the hospital. If they get nervous or worried, your art will remind them that God protects them with his peace.**

Ask: • **What are some ways God might protect our hearts when we're worried?**

• **Why would God want us to tell him about the things that worry us?**

Pray: **God, thank you for giving us peace when we're afraid. Please help us remind children that you give us peace. In Jesus' name, amen.**

Washed Clean

Bible Point

God forgives us.

Scripture

"Wash me, and I will be whiter than snow" (Psalm 51:7b).

We've all been in negative situations that draw our entire focus. Those problems often seem so dire that we have a hard time seeing Jesus and growing in a relationship with him. Many people in the community are in some tough places, some of which we can't even fathom. They can't even begin to understand the grace and love offered by Jesus until it is shared with them. Your kids will share Jesus' love with people in your community in a practical way: by making decorative detergent scoops and donating detergent to people living in homeless shelters.

Supplies

- 1 empty detergent scoop per child
- tempera paints
- paint dishes
- 1 paintbrush per child
- 1 cup of water for every 2 or 3 kids
- resealable plastic sandwich bags
- dry laundry detergent
- tape

Steps

1. Give each child a paintbrush and a clean, empty detergent scoop. Direct kids to be creative as they paint the scoops.

2. Set the scoops aside to dry. Help the children fill resealable bags with dry laundry detergent.

3. When the scoops have dried completely, attach them to the bags with tape. Deliver the crafts to a nearby homeless shelter or college dormitory.

Closing

Discuss these questions with your children:

- **How do you feel when you have clean clothes to wear or fresh, clean sheets to sleep in?**

- **How does Jesus help us "clean" up our lives?**

- **How is the feeling of clean sheets or clothes like the feeling we have when Jesus forgives us for our sins?**

Say: **When we ask Jesus to forgive us, we are asking him to help us clean up our hearts so we don't have the dirty sin anymore. We can also share that feeling of being clean with others. When we give others in our community the detergent to wash and clean their clothes, we can tell them about how Jesus cleans them by loving and forgiving them.**

Pray: **Dear God, help us be mindful of those in our community who need help. Help them to know that Jesus loves them and forgives their sins. In Jesus' name, amen.**

Angel Guardians

Bible Point

God sends his angels to protect us.

Scripture

"For he will command his angels concerning you to guard you in all your ways" (Psalm 91:11).

As your kids create these greeting cards, they'll be reminded that God is watching out for them, protecting them with angel guardians. The cards will remind other people, too!

Supplies

- 1 decorative cupcake liner per child
- 1 half sheet of construction paper per child
- 1 heart-shaped sticker ($\frac{1}{2}$- to 1-inch wide) per child
- 1 card-size envelope per child
- crayons or markers
- safety scissors
- glue sticks
- Bible

Steps

1. Give each child a half sheet of construction paper. Then have kids fold their pieces in half.

2. Help kids write the words of Psalm 91:11 on the inside of their cards. While you're helping kids write, ask them to think of something to write to encourage and thank military personnel for serving their country.

3. Give each child one cupcake liner, and tell kids to fold their liners in half and fold the half into equal thirds. Have them unfold the thirds, keeping the liners folded in half, and cut along one fold. Have each child unfold the smaller piece and cut it in half to create two wings. The remaining section, still folded, will form the angel's body.

4 Show kids how to form angels out of the pieces by positioning each small piece as wings and each large piece as the body. The body piece should be refolded so that the cut edges are hidden when glued. Give kids time to glue each section to their cards, allowing the ruffled edges to puff up.

5 To finish the angels, give each child a heart sticker as a face to be placed where the corners of the liner pieces meet.

6 Have kids place the cards in envelopes addressed to military personnel or government leaders known to your church. If your church is in the United States, you may also use this Web site to learn how to send your cards to other U.S. military personnel: www.anysoldier.us. If your church is in another country, consult a military office for information.

Tip

If you have children who have lost loved ones recently, be sensitive to their feelings as you discuss this craft. Explain that we may not know why God allows bad things to happen to people, but we do know that he loves us.

Closing

Say: **When we feel worried or afraid, it helps to remember that God promises to protect us. He gives angels the job of guarding us. Even grown-ups are sometimes in difficult or dangerous situations. Receiving your notes will remind them that God sends his angels to protect us.**

Ask: • **How do we know God's angels are protecting us?**

• **How do you feel knowing that God's angels are protecting you?**

Pray: **Dear God, thank you for sending your angels to guard us. Please watch over members of our military and leaders in our government. Help our notes reach those who most need your encouragement. Amen.**

Badge of Courage

Bible Point

God is on our side.

Scripture

"So do not fear, for I am with you; do not be dismayed, for I am your God. I will strengthen you and help you; I will uphold you with my righteous right hand" (Isaiah 41:10).

Firefighters put out fires. Police officers help those who need help. Both tasks require bravery and courage. As children share their Badge of Courage crafts with firefighters or police officers, they'll be reminded that, with God's help, they can also be brave.

Supplies

- one 6-inch foam plate per child
- 1 chenille wire per child
- aluminum foil
- 1 adhesive label per child
- two 4-inch strips of ¾-inch ribbon per child
- glue
- transparent tape
- box of tissues
- safety scissors
- fine-tipped markers

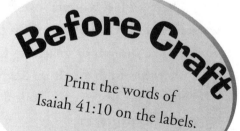

Before Craft

Print the words of Isaiah 41:10 on the labels.

Steps

1. Give each child a chenille wire. Have kids cut them into two-inch and four-inch sections and glue the sections to the front of the foam plate in the shape of a cross.

2. Give each child a 10x12-inch piece of foil. Direct kids to place the foil over their plates and fold the edges

to the back. Ask kids to gently rub the foil with soft tissues or cloths to reveal the shape of the cross on the front of the plates. Tell them to be careful not to tear the foil.

3 Ask kids to each write the word "Courageous" on one strip of ribbon. On the other strip, have each child write the word "Christian."

4 Tell kids to tape the ribbons to the back of their plates so they extend below the edge. Allow them to attach the Scripture labels to the backs.

Closing

Discuss these questions with your children:

- **What are some scary situations you face?**

- **What does it mean to be brave?**

- **What can you tell someone who needs to be brave?**

Say: **We can trust God for courage at school, at home, in the dark, or anytime we feel afraid. God is bigger than all our fears. When we need to be brave, our powerful God will give us courage to do what is right. Share the Badge of Courage with someone who needs to be brave, like a police officer or firefighter, and help that person remember that God will give us courage when we are afraid.**

Pray: **Dear Lord, thank you for never leaving us. Help us be brave and courageous for you. In Jesus' name, amen.**

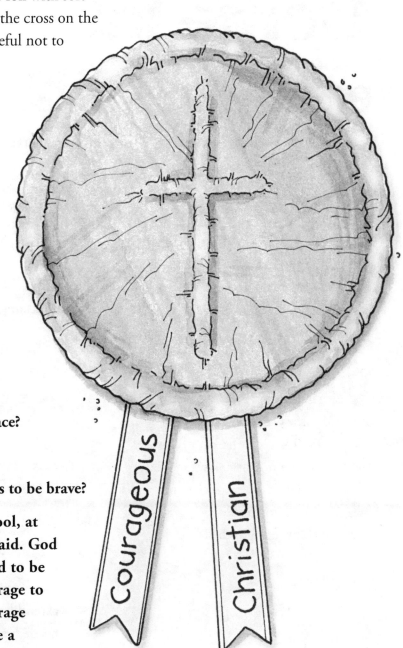

Come In!

Bible Point

Jesus wants to enter our hearts.

Scripture

"Here I am! I stand at the door and knock. If anyone hears my voice and opens the door, I will come in and eat with him, and he with me" (Revelation 3:20).

When someone we know knocks at our door, we answer and let our friend in. Jesus is our friend who wants to live inside our hearts. As they share these door knockers, your children will help others know that Jesus is a good friend who's waiting to be invited in.

Supplies

- 4 large colored craft sticks per child
- 1 regular-sized colored craft stick per child
- one 18-inch piece of yarn per child
- tacky glue
- metallic gel pens
- masking tape
- Bible

Steps

1. Give each child four large craft sticks and one regular-sized craft stick. Have the children each place the four large craft sticks side by side in a vertical position.

2. Using a quick-dry or tacky glue, help the children each attach the regular-sized craft stick in a horizontal position so that it runs perpendicular to the large craft sticks about one inch from the top. The edges should extend beyond the sides of the large craft sticks. If needed, add temporary pieces of masking tape to either side of the craft sticks to secure the sticks during the drying process.

3. While the glue dries, have the children use metallic gel pens to write "Come In" on one side of their door knockers. On the other side, have kids write the

words of Revelation 3:20 vertically. To add a creative touch, let the children think of college students they can give their crafts to. Have them decorate the crafts according to what those people like or do.

4 Direct each child to tie the yarn onto the ends of the horizontal craft stick for hanging and to remove the masking tape when the glue is dry.

Closing

Discuss these questions with your children:

- **What should you do when a friend knocks at your door?**

- **How is someone knocking at the door of your house like Jesus wanting to be a part of your life?**

- **How can you help someone know how to let Jesus into his or her life?**

Say: **The Bible tells us that Jesus loves us and wants to be a part of our lives. Jesus wants us to invite him into our lives and let him be our friend and Savior. Take or send your craft to a college student this week. Invite the college student to hang your door knocker on his or her door to let others know to come on in! Your gift will also be a great reminder to keep Jesus at the center of the student's life.**

Pray: **Dear Jesus, thank you for loving us and wanting to be part of our lives. Help us remember to keep you first. In your name, amen.**

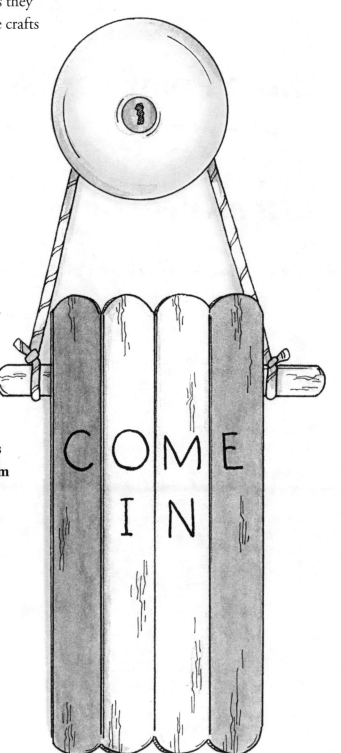

Crazy Creatures

Bible Point

Through Christ, we become new creations.

Scripture

"Therefore, if anyone is in Christ, he is a new creation; the old has gone, the new has come!" (2 Corinthians 5:17).

This craft will help your children see that because God loves them, he wants to give them new life, a life that they'll live forever with him. As children give these crafts away, they can tell those who receive the crafts about new life in God!

Supplies

- 1 craft stick per child
- glue sticks
- colored construction paper
- assorted craft items, such as rickrack, lace, yarn, and wiggle eyes
- scissors
- markers

Steps

1. Give each child a craft stick. Instruct kids to write "Through Christ…" on one side of each stick. Then ask them to write "We are made new!" on the other side of each stick.

2. Have each child cut out a butterfly, bird, ladybug, or other creature from the construction paper, making it about five square inches. Have kids decorate their creatures with the craft items or construction paper.

3. Direct each child to glue his or her creature to the tip of the craft stick.

Closing

Discuss these questions with your children:

- **Have you ever planted a seed and watched it grow? What kind of plant did you grow?**

- **How did it make you feel to watch your plant grow?**

- **What are some ways God helps us grow?**

- **How does it make you feel to know that God loves you so much that he wants to help you grow into a better person, one that will live forever with him?**

Say: **If we let him, God will make us new, and we can live forever with God. This is exciting news that we can share with others. The new creatures we made to go in flowerpots are a great reminder of how God can make us new too! Give your creature to someone who needs to be reminded of God's love this week. You could give it to someone in the hospital or a nursing home, or just stick it in a plant when you visit the dentist!**

Pray: **Dear Jesus, thank you for the chance to tell others how much you love us and want to make us new. Thank you for your love. Amen.**

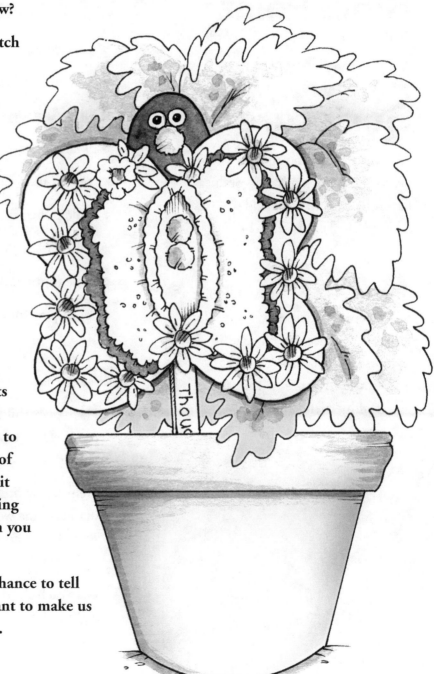

"Fruitful Actions" Mobile

Bible Point

God will fill us with the fruit of his Spirit.

Scripture

"But the fruit of the Spirit is love, joy, peace, patience, kindness, goodness, faithfulness, gentleness and self-control" (Galatians 5:22-23).

As your children make this craft to be viewed by patients in a doctor's or dentist's office, they'll be reminded that just as fruit helps keep our physical bodies healthy, spiritual fruit is a sign of a healthy friendship with Jesus.

Supplies

- colored paper
- colored markers or glitter colored markers
- safety scissors
- 9 large fruit-shaped stencils
- ten 18-inch lengths of white thread per child
- hole punch
- 1 brightly colored disposable plastic bowl per child
- tape (optional)
- push pin (for leader use)

Steps

1. Have each child trace nine pieces of fruit onto colored paper. Then have kids cut out the fruit and punch a hole in the top of each fruit shape.

2. Help kids write the following words on the fruit with markers, one word per fruit shape: *love, joy, peace, patience, kindness, goodness, faithfulness, gentleness,* and *self-control.*

3. Give each child a plastic bowl, and help kids punch eight holes around the rim of each bowl at equal distances.

4 Use a push pin to poke two holes, about one-fourth inch apart, in the bottom of each child's bowl.

5 Give each child ten pieces of string. Direct kids to tie one end of each piece of string to a fruit shape. Show kids how to tip the bowls upside down and tie the other ends of the string around the bowls. Remind them to let each piece of fruit hang at various lengths. Have them each tie the last piece of string through the two holes in the bowl's base for hanging. Kids may add tape to reinforce string, if desired.

Closing

Say: **"But the fruit of the Spirit is love, joy, peace, patience, kindness, goodness, faithfulness, gentleness and self-control"** (Galatians 5:22-23). **Just as real fruit can be healthy for our bodies, the fruit of the Spirit can show others that we have a healthy friendship with Jesus. Your "fruit of the Spirit" mobiles will be a special comfort to people who are seeing the dentist or doctor.**

Ask: • **How can we help others see Jesus?**

• **What is one thing you can do to show one fruit of the Spirit in your life?**

Pray: **Dear Jesus, thank you for the chance to comfort others. Help us show them the way to you. Amen.**

Givey Bank

Bible Point

God wants us to share what he has given us.

Scripture

"Each man should give what he has decided in his heart to give, not reluctantly or under compulsion, for God loves a cheerful giver" (2 Corinthians 9:7).

Imagine having a room full of games, toys, clothes, and lots of dollar bills. Now imagine that it was all yours—to give away. Would giving it away be as much fun as keeping it? God gives us everything we need and more. He wants us to gladly share what we have with others. Creating these Givey Banks and placing them near vending machines or on a counter in a workplace will provide others with an opportunity to consider ways to cheerfully give.

Supplies

- 1 small snack can with a plastic lid, such as a Pringles can, per child
- wide masking tape
- 1 can of brown or black solid shoe polish for every five children
- 2 plastic sandwich bags per child
- 1 large paper plate per child
- sharp knife (adult use only)
- protective clothing
- newspapers

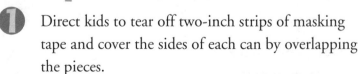

Before Craft

Use a sharp knife to make a $\frac{1}{4}$ x $1\frac{1}{2}$-inch slit in the lid of each can. To protect children's clothes, provide smocks or simple plastic bags for kids to wear. Protect the work area with newspaper.

Steps

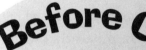 Direct kids to tear off two-inch strips of masking tape and cover the sides of each can by overlapping the pieces.

2 When the sides of the can are completely covered, give each child a paper plate and two sandwich bags to use

as mitts. Direct kids to put their cans on the plates. Instruct the children to each spread a very light coat of shoe polish over the tape. This will give it a leathery look.

 Have the kids attach the lids and set the crafts aside to dry.

Closing

Discuss these questions with your children:

- **What kinds of things has God given you?**
- **What has God asked us to do with the things he has given us?**
- **What should our attitude be when we give?**
- **In what ways can we share God's gifts?**

Say: **God wants us to show our love for him by sharing what he has given us. Second Corinthians 9:7 says, "Each man should give what he has decided in his heart to give, not reluctantly or under compulsion, for God loves a cheerful giver." Just as we receive things from God, we should also happily share those things with others. When your can is dry, use a marker to write on it that you will give this money to someone in need. Be the first to add some coins to your Givey Bank, then ask someone to place it where others can give. When it's full, give the money you've collected to someone in need. As you share your Givey Bank, remember to also share God's best gift—Jesus!**

Pray: **Dear Jesus, thank you for giving us so much. Teach us to gladly share with others. In your name, amen.**

"Rainbow of Light" Tags

Bible Point

We can help others see Jesus.

Scripture

"Let your light shine before men, that they may see your good deeds and praise your Father in heaven" (Matthew 5:16).

God's light shines through our good deeds. As people reach for the switches these crafts will be attached to, they will see the light of Christ shining into their lives!

Supplies

- one 10-inch square of white poster board per child
- glow-in-the-dark markers or pens
- 1 ball chain per child, at least 6 inches in length
- hole punch
- safety scissors
- glow-in-the-dark puffy paint
- glue

Steps

1. Give each child a square of white poster board, and have kids each cut out a rainbow shape at least six inches wide.

2. Direct kids to each cut half of a sunshine shape out of the poster board and color it yellow.

3. Allow kids to decorate their rainbows with the glow-in-the-dark markers.

4. Have kids glue the sunshine shapes to the back of the rainbows so the sun is peeking over the top. Help them write "Let your light shine" on each sunshine shape with puffy paints.

5. Have each child punch a hole at the top of the rainbow and attach a chain through the hole.

Closing

Discuss these questions with your children:

- **What is so important about light?**

- **How is a joyful attitude like light?**

- **How can our joyful attitude help others see Jesus?**

Say: **Light helps people see different things. God wants us to be like lights so others can see him. The Bible says, "Let your light shine before men, that they may see your good deeds and praise your Father in heaven" (Matthew 5:16). This rainbow lamp ornament is one way we can light the way to Jesus for others!**

As a class, give your light-switch tags to a group home in the area. Ask the group-home staff to attach the tags to lamps in their home as reminders of Christ's light in their lives.

Pray: **Dear Lord, thank you for filling us up with your light. Please help us let our light shine each day for you. We pray that our lamp ornaments will shine light for others to see you. In Jesus' name, amen.**

Rays of Hope

Bible Point

God can guide us through life.

Scripture

"And we know that in all things God works for the good of those who love him, who have been called according to his purpose" (Romans 8:28).

God has a purpose and calling for each one of us, and even our ordinary days can be extraordinary if we allow God to guide our lives. As they make this craft, your children will learn that God can take the ordinary and make it extraordinary and beautiful.

Supplies

- 1 clear deli-container lid per child
- permanent colored markers
- hole punch
- one 18-inch length of ribbon per child

Steps

1. Give each child a deli lid, and help each child punch a hole in the edge.

2. Have kids tie one piece of ribbon through each hole for hanging.

3. Have the children carefully use permanent markers to design patterns on the lids and color them in.

Closing

Discuss these questions with your children:

- **What are some yucky things that happen in our lives?**

- **How do we know that God is still in control during those bad times?**

- **Why does God use us to help others know him?**

- **In what ways can God use you?**

Say: **The Bible says, "And we know that in all things God works for the good of those who love him, who have been called according to his purpose" (Romans 8:28). Sometimes it seems as if our lives are really boring or even yucky. But just as we made the boring deli lids look pretty, God can use our yucky days and make something good happen. When we let God shine through us, he can do beautiful things. Each one of our lives is special and can be used by God. Give your sun catchers to people who need to be reminded that God wants to be a guide for their lives.**

Pray: **Dear Jesus, thank you for being a light and a guide in our lives. Help us follow you every day. Amen.**

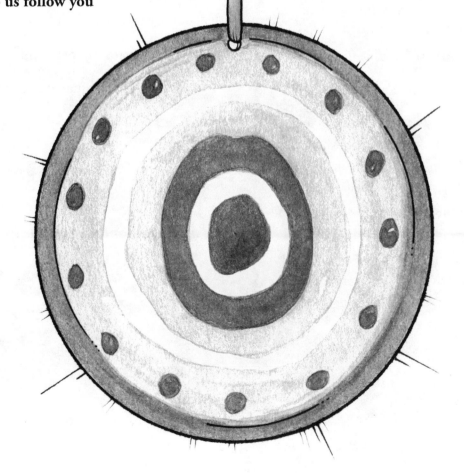

"Say and Do" Memo Pad

Bible Point

Please God in all you say or do.

Scripture

"And whatever you do, whether in word or deed, do it all in the name of the Lord Jesus, giving thanks to God the Father through him" (Colossians 3:17).

There are many things we have to remember to do each day. Sometimes people make lists to help their memories. Whatever we do and say should be for pleasing God and showing our thankfulness to him. Children will create memo pads to share with people as reminders to please God in everything.

Supplies

- 1 file folder for every three children
- paper
- 1 container of water-based decoupage sealer (such as Mod Podge)
- crayons or markers
- 2 paper clips per child
- 1 cotton swab per child
- one 2-inch-square paper or adhesive label per child

Before Craft

Print the words of Colossians 3:17 on the labels. Measure seven inches from the folded edge of each folder, and cut out three 3x7-inch mini folders, using both sides of the folder. Cut paper into 2¾x6½-inch strips. You'll need sixteen strips for each child.

Steps

 Give each child sixteen strips of paper, and direct kids to stack their paper and tap the narrow edge on the table to make it flush. Have each child attach a paper clip at one long side to hold the papers together.

 Instruct kids to each use a cotton swab to spread a generous amount of decoupage sealer along the flush edge of the paper and a small amount in the crease of the folder. Allow kids to each press the glued edge of paper into the folded edge of the folder. Have each child secure the pad on the outside with another paper clip until completely dry (about ten minutes).

 As the decoupage sealer dries, let the children decorate the outside of the notepads and then attach the verse labels and decorate them.

Closing

Discuss these questions with your children:

- **If you made a list of things to do today that would please God, what would be on it?**

- **What should our attitude be toward everything we do and say?**

- **How can we please God through the things we do and say?**

Say: **People write down important things they need to do. Sometimes they make shopping lists or write down jobs that need to be done. God wants us to remember that whatever we do, we should do it to please him. The next time you go to the store with a family member, give your memo pad to someone standing in line, and remind that person to please God with a thankful heart in all he or she does.**

Pray: **Dear Jesus, help us show our love for you by being careful to only do and say things that please you. Amen.**

"Standing Firm" Pencil Holder

Bible Point

We glorify God when we stand firm in our work for him!

Scripture

"Therefore, my dear brothers, stand firm. Let nothing move you. Always give yourselves fully to the work of the Lord, because you know that your labor in the Lord is not in vain" (1 Corinthians 15:58).

The shoe-shaped pencil holders your children make will be constant reminders that all work is to be done as unto the Lord.

Supplies

- 3 ounces of no-bake modeling clay per child
- 1 toothpick per child
- one 1x2-inch piece of white card stock or construction paper per child
- fine-tipped colored markers
- hole punch
- one 6-inch piece of colorful plastic string per child

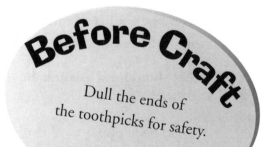

Before Craft

Dull the ends of the toothpicks for safety.

Steps

1. Give each child three ounces of clay (about a handful). Show the children how to mold the clay into shoes about three to four inches long, one inch thick at the toe, and three inches tall at the heel. Tell the kids to each leave a hole at the ankle area for pencils.

2. Give each child a toothpick. Tell kids to make two holes in the top front part of each shoe for shoelaces.

3. Give each child a piece of white card stock. Ask kids to punch a hole in the top of each piece and write

"Stand firm as you work for the Lord" on it with markers.

 Give each child a piece of plastic string. Help each child thread the string through the two holes, attach the message onto the string, and tie a bow.

Closing

Discuss these questions with your children:

- **Who are some people you know who do their work for the Lord?** (Remind kids that these people may not necessarily work for a church.)

- **What are some things *you* might do to serve God?**

- **What kind of attitude should we have as we work in ways that honor God?**

Say: **God wants all of us to stand firm with him in everything we do. The Bible says, "Therefore, my dear brothers, stand firm. Let nothing move you. Always give yourselves fully to the work of the Lord, because you know that your labor in the Lord is not in vain" (1 Corinthians 15:58). As we give our pencil holders to others, we'll encourage those people to continue to stand firm with God in everything they do at work.**

Pray: **Dear Lord, thank you for giving each one of us special jobs to do for you. As we give this craft away, we pray that it will be an encouragement to others as they do their work for you. Please help us, Lord, to stand firm in all the work we do for you too! In Jesus' name, amen.**

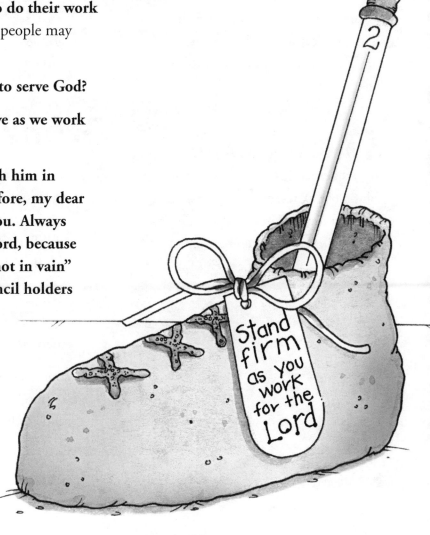

"Wonderfully Made" Posters

Bible Point

God made us.

Scripture

"I praise you because I am fearfully and wonderfully made; your works are wonderful, I know that full well" (Psalm 139:14).

Our bodies are amazing! Our hearts beat, our lungs expand, and our blood circulates, even when we don't think about it. These crafts will remind your children and members of your church that God made each of us a unique child.

Supplies

- 1 large sheet of newsprint per child (big enough for the child to lie on)
- pencils
- crayons or markers
- Bible

Steps

1. Tell kids to do this activity in pairs. Ask one partner to lie on his or her back on a sheet of newsprint while the other uses a pencil to trace around the child's outline. Then have children switch roles, using another sheet of newsprint.

2. Tell kids to use markers or crayons to draw a heart shape in the center of each outline. Ask kids to write the words of Psalm 139:14 inside each heart.

3. Encourage kids to decorate their outlines to look like themselves. Suggest that kids add hair, facial features, and clothes.

4. Make sure kids write their names on their paper people.

Closing

Discuss these questions with your children:

- **What does it mean to be "fearfully and wonderfully made"?**

- **How do you feel knowing that God made you?**

- **How can you praise God this week?**

Say: **Each of us is a walking miracle. Think about it—no one except God can create a person. He made each of us who we are. Let's hang our posters along the halls of the church to remind everyone that God made us—and them!**

Pray: **Dear God, thank you for the miracle of life. Thank you for making us, for knowing us, and for loving us. Help us remember each day what a loving Father you are. And please help us tell others about you too. In Jesus' name, amen.**

Bible Point Index

Bible Verse Index